Praise for *The Blind Spot Effect*

"Kelly Boys explores powerful new science about the important things we miss each day—and the simple, practical things we can do to see the good news about ourselves and the world that's right under our noses. In an informal and friendly style, she helps us see the unseen, shed needless stress and worries, and open into something quite profound."

RICK HANSON, PHD
New York Times bestselling author of
Buddha's Brain and *Resilient*

"*The Blind Spot Effect* is a fresh and illuminating take on how to step out of lifelong patterns that keep snagging us . . . highly recommended!"

TARA BRACH, PHD
author of *Radical Acceptance* and *True Refuge*

"We all have blind spots, and this book expertly reveals how mindfulness and emotional intelligence training can help us see clearly and stop the mental and emotional suffering we create in our own lives. When we start within, we can make peace in the world. This book is an essential starting point for discovering that peace within ourselves, which is bound to have ripple effects with our families and at work, as well as out into the larger global community."

CHADE-MENG TAN
Google pioneer and *New York Times* bestselling author
of *Joy on Demand* and *Search Inside Yourself*

"In *The Blind Spot Effect*, Kelly Boys skillfully reveals profound insights into our own conditioning and lays out a path to positive change in our lives. A deeply helpful look at this underexplored topic."

SHARON SALZBERG
author of *Real Happiness* and *Real Love*

D03390854

"For us to live in this world, we create a narrative that allows us to respond to the vagaries of our life and it is created early on. Most of us are unaware such a narrative exists. It is this narrative that often creates blind spots that negatively affect relationships and our ability to achieve, and is a source of unhappiness. Kelly Boys shows us our blind spots and by doing so allows us to truly see. When we truly see, everything changes for the better."

JAMES R. DOTY, MD
founder and director of The Center for Compassion and Altruism Research and Education at Stanford University, and *New York Times* bestselling author of *Into the Magic Shop: A Neurosurgeon's Quest to Discover the Mysteries of the Brain and the Secrets of the Heart*

"*The Blind Spot Effect* offers us an open window into understanding how to transform our everyday assumptions and beliefs that otherwise create blind spots within us, so that we may live in ever-increasing authenticity and connectedness with ourselves, others, and the world around us. Kelly Boys strikes a perfect balance between her warm and welcoming writing style, the information she offers us regarding the latest research and neuroscience on how our mind creates blind spots, and easy-to-follow exercises."

RICHARD MILLER, PHD
author of *iRest Meditation: Restorative Practices for Health, Resiliency, and Well-Being* and *Yoga Nidra: A Meditative Practice for Deep Relaxation and Healing*

"In very direct, clear, and practical terms that are grounded in neuroscience and psychology, author Kelly Boys shares insights from her many years of experience as an international mindfulness, emotional, and social intelligence teacher and coach. This book is an essential guide that no doubt will move readers down the sometimes difficult—but always fruitful—lifelong journey toward personal and professional growth and fulfillment."

RICHARD FERNANDEZ, PHD
CEO of Search Inside Yourself Leadership Institute

"Blending cutting-edge cognitive research and creative mindfulness practices, Kelly Boys leads us in a lively discovery process through our blind spots toward the core of who we really are as open, loving awareness. *The Blind Spot Effect* is a spirited, fun, and illuminating read!"

JOHN J. PRENDERGAST, PHD
author of *In Touch: How to Tune in to the Inner Guidance of Your Body and Trust Yourself*, retired adjunct professor of psychology at the California Institute of Integral Studies

THE
BLIND
SPOT
EFFECT

THE BLIND SPOT EFFECT

HOW TO STOP
MISSING WHAT'S
RIGHT IN FRONT OF YOU

KELLY BOYS

sounds true
BOULDER, COLORADO

Sounds True, Inc.
Boulder, CO 80306

This book is not intended as a substitute for the medical recommendations of
physicians, mental health professionals, or other health-care providers. Rather,
it is intended to offer information to help the reader cooperate with physicians,
mental health professionals, and health-care providers in a mutual quest for
optimal well-being. We advise readers to carefully review and understand
the ideas presented and to seek the advice of a qualified professional before
attempting to use them.

Some names and identifying details have been changed to protect the privacy
of individuals.

Cover design by Jennifer Miles
Book design by Beth Skelley

Printed in Canada

Library of Congress Cataloging-in-Publication Data
Names: Boys, Kelly, author.
Title: The blind spot effect : how to stop missing what's right in front of you /
    Kelly Boys.
Description: Boulder, Colorado : Sounds True, [2018] |
    Includes bibliographical references.
Identifiers: LCCN 2017058112 (print) | LCCN 2017059928 (ebook) |
    ISBN 9781622039982 (ebook) | ISBN 9781622039975 (pbk.)
Subjects: LCSH: Self-perception. | Self-consciousness (Awareness) |
    Mindfulness (Psychology)
Classification: LCC BF697.5.S43 (ebook) | LCC BF697.5.S43 B69 2018 (print) |
    DDC 158—dc23
LC record available at https://lccn.loc.gov/2017058112

10 9 8 7 6 5 4 3 2 1

This book is dedicated to anyone willing to take a deep breath and plunge like an arrow, headfirst, into the emerald water of *you*. May you resurface with a gasp for air and a delighted giggle, sandy coral treasure in hand, having wriggled free of something serious and profound as if discovering the punch line of a silly and hilarious joke. And this book is for Anne: thanks for laughing with me into and through all the deep dives and discoveries, and for living in Banff, where the mountains loom high and the forests carpet the landscape with their quiet magic.

CONTENTS

INTRODUCTION

◠

*I'm here to be me, which is taking
a great deal longer than I had hoped . . .*
ANNE LAMOTT[1]

EVER SINCE I was a girl I wanted to work in prisons. Not with the psychopaths—that is beyond my pay grade—but your run-of-the-mill felon feels like family to me. The kind of family you don't know what to do with. But you recognize that in some way they never got what they needed, and if they could have a taste of it, you see the possibility of change and a new life.

My favorite thing about going into San Quentin State Prison—where I spent a few years teaching a weekly meditation class—was the kinship I shared with the people inside. As I walked across the prison yard among inmates jogging the track or crouched along the concrete perimeter in the California sun, I felt a sense of heightened alertness, but I was not scared to be there. That's because I have been on the receiving end of violence and have firsthand experience with its dimensions and contours, which we all carry in some form inside ourselves, whether it's acted upon or not. And I know I can show up with a fierce heart and compassionate boundaries. Some of these prisoners were the hyperbolic and unfortunate perpetrators of that shadow of hatred and anger, and some were the reflection of a racially divided, punitive system serving the privileged and punishing the innocent.

Most of the folks I worked with—lifers with the possibility of parole—were incarcerated for acting out of a blind spot. Often, the consequences were deadly. Most of the inmates I spoke with shared that the act that brought them to prison happened in mere seconds, with almost no forethought. When I asked a large circle of men to add up the length of their sentences, it totaled hundreds of years. The crimes that got them there? *The total was minutes.*

I've always had a knack for finding blind spots—the stuff we can't see about ourselves that has an impact on everyone we encounter. These hidden parts that drive us can be transformative in their revelation. I'm drawn to discovering, exploring, and even flailing around in my own and other people's blind spots because I've always been curious about how we can *not* see something that may be blatantly (and at times painfully) obvious to others.

Blind spots, as I define them, are unconscious impulses, fueled by emotions and beliefs, that create habit-building patterns in relationship to ourselves and others. For instance, an inmate who can't quite understand how his self-victimizing behavior keeps landing him behind bars and always blames someone else. Or an insecure person who talks too much and too fast so that everyone he meets thinks, *Wow . . . this dude is trying to prove something. When's he going to be quiet?*

> **Blind spots, as I define them, are unconscious impulses, fueled by emotions and beliefs, that create habit-building patterns in relationship to ourselves and others.**

Blind spots are tricky because we can't see them; their nature is to hide in plain sight. They may lead us to feel depressed or misunderstood, to unknowingly alienate those we love, or to not recognize our own value and power. Blind spots start wars and break up families. They foster disconnection and isolation at home and at work. They hold us back or force us into places we never wanted to be. We may think they're having minor or negligible impacts on our lives but those impacts add up, keeping us from being fully happy, alive, and creative.

Blind spots are *not* the things we already know about ourselves that we are working on, like being more patient with our children or more confident in social situations. Blind spots are *not* abstract ideas. They are ingrained beliefs and attendant emotions that drive us to play out patterns we don't see, all to avoid the obvious that is right in front of us. Who hasn't failed at something or been shocked by someone's behavior and asked themselves, *How did I not see this coming?*

Blind spots can make messes of our lives, yet they also reveal important messages if we are open to examining them. Even when the thing we're discovering is embarrassing or feels shameful, the act of seeing it can be life changing, especially when we see it along with trusted friends or within a safe context for learning and growth. Seeing blind spots is like a treasure hunt—but *not* a witch hunt. If we approach the subject with curiosity and affection rather than shaming ourselves, we can discover some immensely valuable truths.

It was the revelation of my own blind spots that led me to write this book. I've been studying the human condition like a scientist, albeit imprecisely, for two decades. I've taught meditation and emotional intelligence not only in prisons, but in a variety of places including veterans' hospitals, the Google campus, United Nations agencies, and on the front lines of conflict in the Middle East. I've come to realize that cinderblock prison walls, Silicon Valley corporate walls, and the walls of refugees' tents have a lot in common. They all hold passionate, vulnerable human beings who want to have their basic needs met, to be loved and accepted by their families and communities, and to share their gifts with the world. They also hold people who are trying to get ahead even when that means trying (at times desperately) to portray and defend a false image of themselves—an image they are blind to—in order to not be attacked, blamed, or judged.

If you think about it, what do we all want deep down? Dr. Richard Miller, psychologist and founder of the Integrative Restoration Institute, once told me, "Every single person who has come into my office for the past thirty years has come here asking different forms of the same fundamental question: 'Am I okay? Can you tell me that I'm okay?'" What we share is a natural drive for acceptance and love. We are compelled to ask the world to reflect our worthiness back to us as a way of escaping from what is smack dab in front of our faces: our own discomfort in the form of unworthiness, shame, doubt, vulnerability, and all the ways we don't love and accept ourselves as we are.

I've discovered that each of us has at least a few wacky and creative ways of going about getting these needs met. There is nothing wrong with such strategies per se. But the related behaviors can be created and maintained by blind spots. Blind spots that are obvious to others while we, oblivious, coast through life never finding what we're looking for and leaving a wake of unmet needs behind us. Nobody is exempt.

Here's how I discovered a blind spot of my own: I was sitting in a session with a therapist named Paul on a well-used couch in the trendy Mission District of San Francisco, staring at the antique toy fire trucks placed along his windowsill and balancing a glass of water in my lap. A friend had suggested that . . . *just maybe* . . . therapy would be a helpful thing for me to do. I was out of work and ending a relationship, and although I trusted that things were going to turn out okay, I was a bit at sea.

Paul listened to a synopsis of my entire life, including a short foray into my Ohio childhood, my marriage at eighteen and divorce at twenty-one, and a quick trip through twenty years in Germany, Japan, Canada, and England culminating in the Sausalito, California, café where I thought I was going out for a coffee and ended up getting fired. Then he studied me through his tortoise shell–framed glasses and asked, "Do you want to look at your blind spot or do you want to let these patterns repeat?"

Boom!

That was it—that was the question that changed everything for me. I spoke from the depths of my being, and with trepidation and an unsuppressed laugh, when I replied, "*Yes.* Hell, yes." In that moment, I was ready to hear my therapist's words.

When you've been on the receiving end of random, difficult, or sometimes horrible life events, you develop a bullshit detector for people who blame the victim. *This was not that.* This was an honest and genuine question pointing out my own participation in my life patterns. I was undefended and ready to learn something new, ready to grow. I trusted that shining a light on my blind spots would be good and productive, although probably painful.

Up until that moment I had taken a random and fateful approach to the happenings and events in my life—shit happens, good stuff happens, and it's how you navigate it all that matters. I had never thought of my hidden traits in this way before: so pointedly, urgently, and globally. I'd done plenty of work on my emotional life, like setting free self-limiting beliefs and getting in touch with self-compassion and self-trust through mindfulness meditation, but none of this had revealed Paul's insight that something I wasn't seeing *at all*—a blind spot—was driving my behavior. He helped me recognize that what I was missing was just past the edge of my own perceptual horizon. Realizing that this stuff was obvious to someone I'd just met, stuff that had been entirely out of view to me, woke me up. *What had I been missing?*

What I discovered, with Paul's gentle nudging, was that my biggest blind spot had to do with accommodating *other people's blind spots*. I had "protected" certain important people in my life from the impact of their own unconscious behavior—that is, until I finally couldn't take it anymore and blurted out their blind spots. That's where the trouble happened; my unexpected and uncharacteristic speaking of the truth rarely went over well. In fact, it's how I ended up in that coffee shop in Sausalito, shocked when I was let go from my job.

I know I'm not alone. Why is it that so many of us often suffer for no clear reason? What are the patterns (especially those we can't perceive) that interrupt our healthy and sane functioning? Why are we all trying so darn hard to defend our ideas, self-images, and opinions even when doing so hurts us and the people around us? What is at stake here?

It turns out that *everything* is at stake. We are biologically wired for survival, and as humans we have developed a belief that our survival is contingent upon this thing called "me" at the center of our world. To sustain our sense of self, get the love we want, and succeed in our vocations, we engineer all kinds of crafty ways to keep our self-image not only intact, but impervious to attack. There's nothing wrong with that; it's natural . . . except that it's also *not* natural because we're defending an idea instead of something real. To make matters even more interesting, we develop lifelong beliefs that keep us from seeing any of this, *including those beliefs*. If what we want is to be accepted and loved, and to flourish, this doesn't work.

What if seeing our blind spots could radically transform the way we live, work, and perceive reality? Have you ever looked at an optical illusion and been startled or scared to discover what your brain does to make sense of what you're seeing? For instance, you see a gray box even though it's actually white because of how it's positioned on a checkered background, or you see a triangle in a diagram where there isn't one because of strategically placed wedges and angles. Optical illusions point to how easy it is to fill in what we "see" based on memory, the biology of vision, and our brain's need for coherence, and they reveal how much our minds can trick us. Because we perceive the world with relative accuracy most of the time, we're surprised when we get duped. We believe that our senses are exact, so it shocks us when we find out that is not the case. It's the same with uncovering blind spots—and there lies the possibility for life-changing insights to appear.

Something I'll refer to later in this book as well is a visual phenomenon called "attentional blink": a momentary blindness that causes us to miss an object in our field of vision. Not only do our unconscious processes make us see things that aren't there (as optical illusions reveal), but we also blink out on what *is* there! Not that we should see everything; that would be a nightmare. Doesn't it make you wonder, though: with all this blindness—our unconscious beliefs and driving emotions, and even what we miss and make up visually—how do we know which things are worth seeing, and if they even should be seen? Is it possible to illuminate something we are missing that will not only help us be more insightful, but perceive ourselves and the world around us in a whole new way?

Our attention may be our most valuable human resource, and it's something that our inner processes and the world around us compete for: think of how much money is spent on marketing and advertising—on gaining and sustaining our attention. The more overstimulated we get, the more fragmented and partial our attention becomes, pulled in a thousand directions and going in none, and we end up blinking past what is most important, sometimes even if it's right in front of our eyes. If we were to see *more* that is right in front of and within us, would it contribute to the sensory overload we already experience? My theory is that if we illuminate the right things at the right time, they can *reduce* the noise or stimulation in our minds and help us navigate life. When we see something important that we missed, or we stop seeing something that's not there, we gain access to those aspects of power, truth, and authenticity that we have pushed down in favor of the status quo. That's when we begin to align with the natural current of life rather than resisting it. We get unstuck.

Often, self-improvement paths we embark on to "find our purpose" or "live life fully" can be like getting on a hamster wheel that goes nowhere. Such things can be useful but can also be too focused on an unreachable perfection or idealized destination rather than on each step and moment of the journey. Important: *seeking out blind spots is not a self-improvement project*. It's a conversation and process that brings us important perceptions and understanding of the beautiful mess of our lives, not an idealized state. And it's precisely that beautiful mess that holds our happiness.

The purpose of this book is to help you to stop missing what's right before your eyes, uncover your blind spots, and free up energy for your life. More than that, I'd love for this book to shine a light on what we all have in common. Facing our own fallibilities makes it easier to understand those of others. Opening to our vulnerable and caring heart amid life's challenges can ease the sense of separation and heal our inner and outer conflict, bringing us closer to those we love most.

The world is in desperate need of a next step—a different way to approach the same old problems. I believe one of the best things we can do is to illuminate what keeps us from being close to ourselves and close to each other, and to stand together in diverse communities and reclaim the ways in which we have allowed bias, reactivity, and the defense of illusions to divide us. We all have blind spots, we all know people with blind spots, and we are all in this together.

1

ATTENTIONAL BLINK

What We Miss and How We Miss It

Attention, if sudden and close, graduates into surprise;
and this into astonishment; and this into stupefied amazement.

CHARLES DARWIN, *The Expression of the Emotions in Man and Animals*[1]

The Elephant in the Room

Most of us are familiar with the expression "the elephant in the room." It refers to something that is obvious to everyone in that room yet unaddressed between them, often because there are cultural or social taboos around speaking directly to it. Like when you're riding the subway and a ranting drunk person stumbles onto the train and everyone pretends they don't notice him. We have all done this. Often, the elephant in the room remains exactly what it is—seen but unacknowledged—because we know there will be some sort of challenge to face if we name it. Since we're sometimes unprepared to deal with that challenge, it can be easier to leave the elephant in the "pretend shadow"—and in fact sometimes that's the wisest response.

But have you ever stopped to think that you may be avoiding your own elephant? That you may have a blind spot that is obvious to everyone in the room except you? Your response may be to say to yourself, *I've never thought of that! I'm horrified at the possibility that I'm missing something so obvious to everyone else!* Or you may be thinking, *I don't have any big blind spots, but I sure know a lot of people who do!* Either way, this book is for you.

Uncovering our blind spots means that what we have completely (or mostly) not seen, not known, or not experienced suddenly appears before our eyes like a huge, clumsy (at times), graceful (at times) elephant. That's why we hire psychotherapists, read self-help books, take leadership classes, or ask close friends to be honest with us—so we can focus on the gigantic, noisy, large-eared mammal standing directly in front of us that we somehow manage not to see at all.

Interestingly, it doesn't always seem like a full-sized elephant when we do discover it. It can still be a little hazy or obscured. It can take time to see and understand the fullness of the space our blind spots occupy and the impact they have. But they can be painfully—or gloriously—obvious to others! That's the twist: our blind spot can be clear as day to our loved ones or colleagues, but it might take some time for us to fully understand that it's there, and to see its enormity and its consequences, manifesting as the ways we relate to and influence ourselves and the world around us.

Hallucinations

The simple act of seeing what's there, of finding blind spots, can only happen when our attention is *available* and we're not lost in our stories and ideas or on autopilot. Doing things like continually pushing our agenda during meetings without listening to feedback and then wondering why productivity is slow, or not seeing how our constant busyness distances us from our children or how our insecurity drives us to keep secrets from our partner—all of these result in a lack of intimacy and connection.

"Hallucinations" are what neuroscientist Anil Seth says our brain creates when what we perceive doesn't match what is really there. A professor of cognitive and computational neuroscience at the University of Sussex in England, Seth researches the nature of perception and conscious experience. He studies the brain as a prediction machine: how it combines prior beliefs and expectations with sensory input to come up with its best guesses about what we sense and experience, internally and externally.[2]

If you think about it, human beings have extraordinary capacities to perceive the world and interpret it. Seth's framework of "hallucinations" connects to the mechanisms behind blind spots—how we sometimes don't see what's there but instead what we *expect* to be there—and how that doesn't always coincide with reality. When reality and our expectations match, there's no dissonance. But when they don't match, what do we do? If we prefer our expectations over what we actually experience, we see what we want to see and miss what is there. That is the point where we go blind.

In other words, we "hallucinate" when we allow sensory signals to be blocked by the script in our heads: by what we expect and predict. These hallucinations serve to form core beliefs about ourselves and the world around us that run in the background our whole lives and drive our blinded behavior. What if a huge part of your personality or idea of yourself was based on this kind of a blind spot? Wouldn't you want to find that out?

That's what makes searching for our blind spots so intriguing! We all have varying levels of self-awareness and can examine that awareness across a spectrum: one end being emotional intelligence—aware of our inner body sensations, emotions, thoughts, and able to act from learned wisdom—and the other end being cut off from and clueless about what's going on inside (and around) us. Depending on how in touch we are with our inner and outer environment, we can miss a whole lot.

Think of someone you know who is highly emotionally intelligent—someone you learn things from just by being around them—and then think of someone who is so out of touch with themselves that they tend to bring discomfort or suffering to everyone they meet. That is the spectrum.

We have predictive brains that are constantly guessing at what we are perceiving, and the level of our emotional intelligence depends on how correct those guesses are. In some ways, we are like computer algorithms: simpler than our complex environments yet always learning based on new input. To develop self-awareness, the type of data we take in matters, as does the way we approach it. That's why one person can listen to their team at work and find creative ways to solve complex problems while another keeps repeating an inefficient strategy born out of a hallucination that they have the solution and everyone else needs to shut up and follow their orders. The two people are sorting and processing information in different ways, and they may have radically different stories and interpretations of the same problem, which leads to a huge gap in the outcome.

In other words, how sophisticated our learning is depends on how we take in information. We form mental blind spots when we get stuck in a hallucination: in seeing what's not there or in missing what is right in front of us. Optical illusions illustrate that our minds can create something from nothing visually, but this also applies to ideas and beliefs. So the manager who is convinced that his way is correct is missing the fact that the whole team is upset and disengaged because he is seeing something that is not actually there: his infallibility, and their ignorance. These sorts of work scenarios are laborious, stressful, and inefficient. But we can learn to *learn better* when we develop awareness of our brain's tendency to predict what we expect, and hold our own views more lightly, allowing ourselves to be wrong and fallible sometimes. This creates bandwidth for increased curiosity and self-awareness, as well as more meaningful relationships.

Physical Blind Spots

Blind spots don't exist only in our minds. If you've ever driven a car you know that blind spots are actual obscurations in the visual field. We have physical blind spots in our eyes too, called *punctum caecum* in medical literature—an area on our retina that can't detect light because it doesn't have the photoreceptor cells to do so. It's the tiny place where the optic nerve passes into the optic disc. As a result, the corresponding part of the field of vision is invisible to us. We still see what is in front of us without seeing a blank spot in our field of vision—the gap gets filled in by surrounding detail and we don't even know there's something we are missing. (Interestingly, the octopus is the only creature that has no blind spots, due to the placement of its retinal nerve fibers: they don't block light coming in, so the octopus sees everything in front of itself.[3] I like the fact that our blind spots have a literal corollary, but for better or worse, we're not octopuses.) The purpose our physical blind spots serve is to allow us to see everything else in our field of vision. It is in this way that we can acknowledge the importance of blind spots and their function in helping us see.

The same goes for our psychology and how we engage our world: the light is blocked and we miss stuff. Those obscurations were often created when we were young, to help us see other important stuff and to survive and get by okay (just as our physical blind spot means we need to rely on surrounding detail to see the world, our psychological ones helped us navigate life when we were too young to see the whole of our experience). When we're children, we often don't have the tools to cope with the fact that our needs for acceptance, safety, and love aren't getting met, in ways large or small, so we develop creative mechanisms to overlook the hurt and seek out other strategies and behaviors to try to fill our needs. Denial can be a good thing when we're under stress and don't have the tools to cope with our experience, but it's not great when it becomes a habit. It creates a breeding ground for blind spots, and if we don't see them they can hang around for our whole lives, driving our behavior without our knowledge.

The good news about psychological blind spots is that we can bring them into the light, creating the attentional equivalent of photoreceptor cells where we didn't have them before, coaxing our blind spots out of the shadows and into view. Once we recognize our blind spots, we can't *un-see* them again. They're no longer hidden; we're no longer blind; we've awakened from the hallucination and can see the elephant in the room. If we know how to mine them for their gifts, we then have a chance to discover their hidden messages and learn and grow. Blind spots, then, aren't "bad" things about ourselves but are instead helpful puzzle pieces of information in our field of awareness that, when seen, offer a fuller view of what is accurately there. We can learn to perceive light where there is shadow—that is, if we're brave (or crazy) enough.

Attentional Blink

The main reason we don't see the elephant in the room is that there is a gap between what we experience consciously and unconsciously. These gaps on the spectrum of self-awareness are places where our attention "blinks out." Like when we're talking on the cell phone while driving and miss an exit on the freeway, or when we thoughtlessly delete a calendar notification and miss a meeting. We all miss stuff, especially the stuff that lurks beneath the surface of our conscious awareness.

Attention helps us sort, process, and choose what is important and interesting in our environment, and it allows us to omit what is irrelevant. It's hard to focus on more than one thing at a time, even though we like to think of ourselves as good multitaskers. *Attentional blink* is a scientific term for the distance or interval in time (often just a flash) that occurs when our attention moves from one thing to another. It describes *what we miss*, and is a phenomenon based on research about the brain resources we mobilize or have available to us to catch (or miss) information related to the visual field.[4]

In the same way that we hallucinate and filter the world through stories that aren't real, we also miss actual physical objects that are right in front of us, because our attention is elsewhere (like on that trip we are going to take when we retire or the fight we just had with our partner or something we just saw out of the corner of our eye). Attentional blink reveals that beyond our physical blind spot in our retina, we miss actual things in our environment that we *could* see, were our attention freed up to notice it and were it to seem relevant enough to us to remember.

In the 1990s three researchers from the University of Calgary, Jane Raymond, Kimron Shapiro, and Karen Arnell, developed a series of research experiments to test whether people could visually process two letters in a row if one was presented between 180 and 450 milliseconds after the other within a rapidly shown sequence of letters on a computer screen. In one of the experiments, the first letter was a white "T" and the second was a black "X," and the researchers called them both "targets." Raymond and her cohort found that the subjects *often did not* detect the black "X."[5] Since then, there have been many studies examining the nature and possible causes of attentional blink.

Just what was happening during the 180- to 450-millisecond gap? The subjects' attention wasn't freed up to see the second letter because, so the theory goes, their brains were busy identifying the white "T" and didn't have enough time to identify the black "X." That doesn't mean, however, that they didn't *see* the "X."

Raymond and her colleagues posited that we can't quite make something out in our field of vision because our attention is elsewhere, on something like trying to label the white "T," and we minimize the uncertainty and confusion by suppressing what we actually do see—the black "X"—and hence miss it completely. If something is not easy to see and label, we can vanquish it from our experience. *Didn't happen! Nothing to see here!* Sound like a blind spot to you? We miss stuff because we don't have attentional resources to see it: most of us don't recover our attention quickly enough after the first letter to be able to see the second.

Here is where it gets interesting. I have a friend named Chade-Meng Tan. He started his career at Google as an engineer doing "anything that was needed" but specializing in artificial intelligence. Later he became the self-titled "Jolly Good Fellow" and welcomed every famous person under the sun to Google as their ambassador. There's a Wall of Meng that displays photos of him with presidents, prime ministers, actors, and scientists. When I met Meng, these were Polaroid shots, but he's welcomed so many famous people that it's now a revolving digital display!

Enter mindfulness, stage left. Meng, with the help of psychologist Dr. Daniel Goleman, neuroscientist Dr. Philippe Goldin, and meditation teachers Mirabai Bush and Norman Fischer, created an emotional intelligence and mindfulness program for Google engineers called Search Inside Yourself (Get it? It's a play on the Google search function: *you look inside*). The program is a powerful and relevant training that has since gone far beyond the tech world to train industry leaders in the science of what's happening in our minds when we pause, and the impact of this on employee well-being. Meng created it for engineers (it takes one to know one), who tend to have high IQs and . . . um . . . who often need a little help in the emotional intelligence department: defined as self-awareness, self-regulation, motivation, empathy, and social skills (thanks, Dan Goleman, for that formulation!).[6] Self-awareness is the skill that all the others that follow are built upon.

Meng's theory is that to become more emotionally intelligent, we can train our brain using mindfulness to be more aware in the present moment, opening our access to cues in our inner or outer environment. Like: *Oh, he's frowning, he must be upset.* Or: *My stomach is tied up in knots. I think I'm nervous about this project launch. I wonder if we should pause on this to think this through more.* It's catching this data that we would have blinked out on if we were lost in a story or distracted by pressures around us, and then working with it skillfully, that can enhance our well-being and performance at work. When we see through the unnecessary and sidetracking stuff and tune in to more of the salient and relevant stuff, we allow space for our blind spots to be revealed to us.

We hear the term all the time—in advertising, in self-help books—but what is mindfulness?

Attention Training and Insight

Mindfulness, as I'm using it here, is a way of being that is kind and attentive to our own lives—both inner and outer. It helps us train our attention to catch data we typically miss or blink out on; think of it as a pair of glasses we put on so we can filter out what is unnecessary and focus on that elephant in the room. As we slow down in any given moment, we gain access to a high-resolution view that can focus in on any one thing—like an idea or an emotion or something that was unclear to us—while simultaneously including an awareness of the larger context. This keeps us from getting lost in the details and fosters a sense of inclusiveness and kindness toward our experience. It's a powerful tool that has helped me uncover and continue to work with my own blind spots.

Mindfulness has two key components: attention and insight. Building the muscle of attentional focus and capacity to be present with ourselves and our experience can take time because it's easy to zone out and distract ourselves, but it is based on tons of tiny moments building upon each other. Once we can hang out with something—through attention practice (like placing our attention on our breath flowing in and out or the sensations in the palms of our hands or even a difficult emotion)—we become able to stabilize our awareness long enough to ask ourselves honest questions and look with curiosity and clarity into any given situation, question, or problem. This is insight.

PRACTICE Five Mindful Breaths

Since mindfulness is key to this book and to uncovering blind spots, let's jump right in and get some practice in it.

- Sit somewhere comfortable, with your feet on the ground and your hands on your thighs, gazing down. Notice how your feet and hands feel. Are they warm? Cool? Simply sit, aware of your experience as well as your surroundings.

- Feel your spine erect and your posture at ease: both alert and relaxed. Notice how it feels in your body to be awake and alert while also being open and relaxed. Your shoulders may soften and your breath begin to slow down.

- Take five mindful breaths in the following way: As you inhale, be aware of the flow of air into your body through your nose. As you exhale, be aware of the flow of air from your body through your nose.

- Follow your breath in and out four more times; with your eyes open or closed, keep your attention on your breath, following the waves of breath in and out.

- Now allow yourself to reorient to the room and to your surroundings. What do you notice in your experience right now, in this moment? How is it to simply be with your breath in and out? Did your mind race or was it quiet? There is no particular way this needs to look; simply being with your experience as it is, is the practice.

- Voila! You've practiced mindfulness attention training.

As you repeat this practice, you'll see that *how* we do it, not *what* we do—in other words, the *quality* of our attention—is more important than the stuff we are looking at and experiencing. We can feel sad and be in utter resistance to the sorrow, judging ourselves and pushing our emotion down, or we can feel sad and simply be with sorrow as it is, meeting it with compassion and giving it space to be there, feeling curious about it. It's such a radical idea to think that simple qualities like curiosity, kindness, and love—the foundational principles of mindfulness—are key necessities when we face life's challenges. The insight that results when we are with our experience in this way is astounding. Mindfulness is the great undoing: with each moment, we are invited to drop our façade and be real with what is—*right here and now*. It isn't goal oriented; it's presence oriented. It's a way of being with *what is* as we wake up to all the stuff we resist and want to change (including our blind spots). In that sense, mindfulness is a moving target: it's always fresh in the moment, and it's only ever applied in our life in real time. Our attention is a valuable resource that, when paired with this curious, open way of being, can illuminate what is in the shadows.

Now let's get into some of the science of this. It was in Google's engineer-friendly world, while getting to know Meng, that I was first exposed to neuroscience-based research on the efficacy of mindfulness practices. Meng built it into his program at Google because otherwise it's a hard sell to scientific types like engineers that shutting your eyes and doing nothing can be helpful to your life. Rather than mindfulness being some hippie phenomenon, the research points to outstanding benefits: mindfulness meditation can change the structure and function of your brain, with positive impact on all sorts of stuff from physical and mental health to attention regulation and all the way down to improved DNA sequencing.[7]

This brings us back to attentional blink. One of the studies on mindfulness that stood out to me in Meng's Search Inside Yourself program was the attentional blink research by Richard Davidson and his colleagues. Davidson is the founder of the Center for Healthy Minds at the University of Wisconsin–Madison and is a research professor of psychology and psychiatry. He's responsible for a boatload of inquiry into meditation, contemplative practices, and emotional well-being. Davidson and his colleagues scanned and compared the brains of seventeen people who had just spent three months in intensive meditation training—doing practices like the Five Mindful Breaths—with those of twenty-three meditation novices (asked to meditate twenty minutes per day). The task Davidson gave his participants was to successively pick out two numbers in a series of letters, presented in the attentional blink testing style I described earlier.[8] The novices *all* showed attentional blink and missed the second number. In contrast, *all* the trained meditators successfully picked out both numbers. *Wild, right?*

This was replicated in a 2009 study by neuroscientist Sara van Leeuwen at Goethe University Frankfurt.[9] The visual attention of three groups of volunteers was tested: adults around fifty years old with up to twenty-nine years of meditation practice, adults around fifty years old who were not longtime meditators, and young adults who had never meditated before (they added the whippersnappers in to account for their visual acuity in case it made a difference). These participants viewed a series of letters flashed on a screen, with two numbers concealed among them. Volunteers had to name both numbers, and they knew the setup—that the second number was often difficult to see since the first number often masked it. Performance on such attentional speed tests usually declines with age, but the expert meditators outscored both their peers and the younger participants! That's amazing and suggests that if we practice meditation, which is a form of attention training, we have more access to information (in this case, numbers) within our field of awareness and higher efficiency processing that information.

The leap I'm making is that this does not apply just to the visual field, and that mindfulness, along with a few other tools such as inquiry, reflective journaling, and talking to close friends or therapists, can be used to uncover our blind spots and see more clearly what is there. *Everything* is information, in one way or another—our thoughts, emotions, body sensations, visual cues, feelings. Our inner and outer worlds. This is a radical insight. We travel on our own information superhighway and as we become conscious of it we start seeing things . . . like the elephant in the room.

Gorillas in the Room

If you're freaking out now because you want to find your blind spots but don't have time to become an adept meditator like those folks in the research studies, fear not! It's not that cut and dried. I've seen plenty of people without much experience in mindfulness uncover their blind spots. Remember: mindfulness is a way of being kind and attentive to your life, not a thing you do to get somewhere. If anyone stops for a moment and looks at what is coming into focus, or allows space for something to be hazy and is patient with their own process, an insight is likely to emerge. We are wired to learn from what we meet in life, and if we get out of our own way, learning happens naturally.

Amishi Jha, a psychologist and researcher at the University of Miami, studies the impact of mindfulness on attention and working memory in high-stress groups like the military or high-performance athletes to find best practices for resilience and well-being. Typically, our attention and working memory become worse when we are in stressful scenarios (think about the last time you were completely anxious and trying to make an important decision). Jha's research with the University of Miami football team suggests that even four short weeks of mindfulness training protects against the degradation of attention.[10] When I interviewed her, she told me (talking a mile a minute—speaking of brain processing, I think she is way faster than the average human being!) that as opposed to stabilizing our attention on something, when our minds are "wandering," we don't perceive our environment as we normally do. Sounds aren't as loud, light is dimmer, and there is what is called in science a *perceptual decoupling*.

Perceptual decoupling is what happens when you're walking down the street and you stop dead in your tracks because you are thinking hard about something, and you lose contact with what is happening around you. You might not even realize you stopped walking! This can be incredibly positive if you do it intentionally (or not) for creative thinking, but not so much when you're on a football field trying to find the ball. Amishi found that when football players practiced mindfulness training, they were protected against their attention degrading in this way. When I asked Amishi if it was possible that training in mindfulness could help us see blind spots, she exclaimed, "Absolutely! The more stable you can be in your present-moment awareness, the higher the integrity of the information that gets into your brain. When you're not checking out, your 'sampling' of the environment will better impact everything, including emotional reactivity." The key, she says, is practice.

Another example of attentional blink is when we are overly focused on one thing and lose sight of another. A famous selective attention test done by Harvard University has been called the "Invisible Gorilla" experiment.[11] Subjects watch an up-close video of six people playing basketball and are asked to count the number of passes between the three players who are wearing white shirts. During the video, a guy dressed up as a gorilla walks out onto the court, beats his chest, and then walks off camera for a nine-second total appearance. The astonishing discovery was that *half* of the people counting the passes of the players wearing white shirts completely missed the gorilla! I've watched the video myself, and I did see the gorilla because I know the experiment but could easily imagine missing it. That is an example of how blind we can be: missing what is in our field of awareness with no idea of what we missed, because we were paying attention to something else.

Honing our attention to see our blind spots may seem a little scary because of what we might find—like an elephant or gorilla. What do we do with the stuff we start to notice when we pay attention on purpose, mindfully, in the present moment? It's so easy to judge ourselves for what we miss or feel embarrassed when the truth is illuminated. Blind spots can be cringe-worthy! But the unconscious stuff we bring into the light isn't "bad" or "wrong." I can't emphasize this point enough. *The last thing I want is for your inner critic to read this book for you.* Be sure not to make this journey of uncovering blind spots into some huge thing. It can be incremental and easygoing. If you start with small steps, you'll eventually be motivated by the love of what you discover. You're embarking on a series of transformations and a deep inner journey that has its own momentum. This, you can trust.

Welcoming

Before we go any further into the mechanisms and varieties of blind spots, I'd like to frame another foundational concept of this book: *welcoming*. So much of our experience is based on *refusing* our experience. "I don't want it to be this way, and if I allow it to be this way I will not find a solution." That's the belief, right? But do we have to fight reality to win? What if reality always wins? And what if rather than resisting it, we *lean in* and find creative solutions to complex problems? Then we could discover a whole new way of being where we join with our experience and respond in a situation-appropriate and spontaneous way. Welcoming can help with this. It means opening the door to everything we experience—turning nothing away—and learning how to authentically meet our own experience in each moment.

This doesn't mean getting rid of all your boundaries, being a doormat, or being flooded by your experiences. Rather, through this concept of welcoming, you open yourself to *what is* in your experience. You get to sit with those patterns, emotions, and beliefs that have been asking for a little TLC since they formed in your consciousness. So if you're embarrassed, for instance, you allow the feeling to be there even though it feels so . . . embarrassing.

If you approach life with a willingness to be with what you encounter without getting lost in it, it moves gracefully within your experience. That brings more authenticity and aliveness into your interactions, but it necessitates compassion for yourself, those you have affected, and those who have hurt you too. *Bless all our hearts*. When you do this, you free your inner critic: the voice that wants to control and manage your experience so you stay safe, loved, and accepted (and out of blame's way!). And you free your attention, too, to uncover new ways of being, like discovering a new passion or feeling freer interpersonally. These things become possible when your attention is not otherwise occupied with refusing the heck out of your current moment's experience—often through the lens of your blind spot.

I first learned about welcoming from Dr. Richard Miller, a psychologist and meditation teacher who developed and researched a trauma-sensitive meditation process called "Integrative Restoration," or iRest, for military veterans experiencing PTSD and other suffering populations. Welcoming is a style of mindfulness practice that allows us to pause and meet each experience with kind attention—as a primary lens and practice through which to engage the beautiful mess of human life. The way to tune in is through the body: it holds a wealth of information in the form of sensations and intuitions, if we pay attention. I like this approach because it's simple, straightforward, and powerful.

The protocol Richard Miller developed can be taught one-on-one or in groups as a guided practice. Miller and I traveled around the United States training large groups of therapists and yoga teachers in this method. One time, as we worked with Sara, a client who was unsure whether to marry the person she was dating and was at a crisis point with her decision, I was blown away by the insights Richard had and the subtle emotional and energetic cues he could pick up on as we worked with this young woman. As she spoke of her troubles and concerns, he pointedly asked, "What do you experience when you relate this story to us?" and as Sara described her feelings he asked, "Is there any fear here? What do you feel in your belly as you speak? Can you welcome that to be here as it is?"

Sitting in the room with our client, I didn't see the cues Richard was picking up on at all, even though I was right there. I felt nothing in my own belly and I didn't sense any fear in Sara; she was talking about a guy she wasn't that into! Yet in response to Richard's gentle questions—his *welcoming* of what was underneath her concerns—she got in touch with a deep-seated fear that was motivating her decision-making and behavior, something she had not seen before: the fear of losing connection with herself and being engulfed by her partner. To prevent feeling that fear, she had focused on his not being attractive enough to keep her interest. She had been stuck in the situation and was trying to solve it from inside the circumstances and her own story around it; she had lost touch with her deeper motivation and feelings, which were keeping her at a distance from someone she actually loved.

This is how we go blind. Like Sara, we get lost in what feels like a true story, and in doing so we are unable to see the deeper truth. Sara feared intimacy, and rather than being in touch with her real and human fear, she was stuck in a place of judgment about her partner. It helped her stay "safe"—but also blind. It was a belief, but when she questioned it she recognized that it wasn't a reliable belief because it hid that deeper truth. Her body had been giving her clues about the answer, but it was easier to be lost in the story than to do the simple thing of slowing down and feeling and welcoming what was there. *We all do this.*

Like Sara, we each have the capacity to see even our biggest blind spots at any given moment through the rudimentary practices of looking at, seeing, and listening to what is present. Mindfulness practice can help us train our attention to catch stuff, and a lens of welcoming helps us work with it in a kind, open way rather than a "fix-it" mentality. In the search for our blind spots we want to catch emotions, beliefs, and patterns of thinking—the origins of blind spots that we aren't privy to—that will help us track down where we are blind and bring us gifts and messages that are important for us to see. When we understand that we all have them, it becomes less threatening to look, and we discover all sorts of interesting gifts.

After moving through her concerns and having a light shone on her blind spot—judging her boyfriend's appearance to keep from feeling her fear of fully entering the relationship with all of herself—Sara could commit in a way that has been beautiful to witness. She is now deeply attracted to her partner and has a whole new understanding of intimacy and love.

What gifts are you missing because of your blind spots, and how can catching what you blink out on—what you mask through your hallucinations in the form of stories and ideas—help you see better?

YOU SEE IT . . .
BUT YOU DON'T SEE IT

Decoding the Stories in Our Minds

I've never seen a purple cow and never hope to see one.
But I can tell you anyhow, I'd rather see than be one.

GELETT BURGESS[1]

THERE'S A GUY named Bill Dan, an unassuming middle-aged man who does an incredible thing. He balances oddly shaped rocks—often with small ones at the bottom and large, heavy ones at the top—on an uneven sand and stone beach in Sausalito, California. Some of his constructions reach heights of five or more feet! Usually you see people balancing rocks starting with a big one on the bottom and placing increasingly smaller ones on top, but he does the inverse, using every shape and size of rock, from as big as your hand to too heavy for most people to lift without help.

What is equally incredible is how many people dismiss what Dan does, sometimes even angrily shouting at him to stop fooling people, calling him a fraud. Plenty of tourists walk by his work, and some refuse to believe what he's doing is real, even when they see it from a couple of feet away. I used to stand and watch it all happen with a cup of coffee in my hand as part of my weekend morning routine. Dan showed me a photo of a laptop he had astonishingly balanced on the railing of the Golden Gate Bridge for a famous computer company because they wanted to run an advertising campaign featuring his work. In the end, they didn't use it because it just looked Photo-shopped, and nobody understood or could believe how amazing it was.

When I asked Bill how he balanced his rocks, he replied, "It's easy—it's just physics." Then he went on to describe in detail the science of leverage and resistance, leaving me intellectually in the dust.

The Chinese Taoist master Yun Xiang Tseng, of the Wudang lineage of martial arts, uses the same principles in a different way: with his body. He was trained in the mountains of China from a young age in *Crouching Tiger, Hidden Dragon*–style methods, like crossing a creek without touching rocks or water. In other words, to sort of float over the creek. Or so he said! I wouldn't be surprised about the creek thing, and I don't think it would seem like magic either, more like someone who knows how to use scientific principles in surprising ways.

When I studied tai chi with Master Tseng, he taught us how to approach a brick wall as a martial artist—with fluidity, connection, and balance through space. He remarked that what is important is that you "see the wall, but you don't see it." In his tradition, when there is an adversary, like a wall or any other form of obstacle, your job is to acknowledge its presence, but not by looking directly at it or "believing" that it exists and is in your way. If you think, *There is a brick wall, I can't get through*, you are stopped completely, but if you see it while *not* seeing it, other ways of working with the barrier or opponent may appear to you. You aren't changing reality with your mind; rather, by letting go of fixed ideas you are opening to an infinite source of creativity and possibility. It's like life. We get so inured to our blind spots and accustomed to our fixed ideas, both conscious and unconscious, that we miss chances to be surprised and delighted by creative solutions, including ones we never thought possible.

There is something poetic about not always being precise and hyperaware, because it allows for the mystery and beauty that is *life* to present itself in unexpected ways, and it leaves room for the inevitable and beautiful imperfections that make us who we are. How can we work with what appears to be immutable—like the brick wall—or impossible—like balancing a boulder on a pebble—to discover another more creative, more truthful way forward and bring blind spots into the light?

We need to be flexible in our thinking and make room for surprises so we can make use of the potential that lies dormant in our mind and heart. Nowhere is this more obvious than in the ideas we spawn in our minds: our thinking doesn't create reality, but it doesn't always reflect it accurately either. We can stare at a stack of balanced rocks and say, "No, that's not real." It doesn't fit our preconceived ideas about the world. Our fixed ideas, opinions, and thoughts seem so solid and real, even in the face of evidence to the contrary. How can we bring more stuff we miss into the light, like our fixed ideas, and discover what's most real while seeing less of what's *not* there?

One way is to understand the nature of the underlying thinking processes that help us make lightning-fast decisions and divert us from seeing things accurately. The name of the game in our mind's intuition and decision-making behavior is *coherence*. If we have a consistent, rational narrative about what is going on inside or around us, we are likely to believe it's true. We trust our own opinions, don't we? Yet sometimes it's the things that feel the truest that are the falsest—our brick walls or un-balanceable rocks—casting shadows that obscure our blind spots and creativity.

Creating Stories

The value and significance we subconsciously place on safety and security as we navigate just *a single day* in our lives can't be overstated. Our predictive brains make sense of our environment, creating stories with their best guesses based on prior information and incoming sensory information. We see what we expect to see, and that can be helpful or unhelpful—helpful if we expect that our staircase hasn't moved so we can navigate it in the dark and unhelpful if we meet someone new at a café and make an inaccurate flash judgment because they look like the bully at our high school.

We come by it honestly. Humankind has been wired for survival since we were fleeing mastodons. We're still operating with a brain wired to locate threat and maintain our physical safety, and even when we are physically safe, our primal survival system still functions, confirming the stories of our minds that help us understand and navigate the complex and chaotic world around us. We have what is called "negativity bias": we are wired to learn from what is negative in our environment (what we consider a threat to our survival) and we aren't wired to learn from what is positive in our environment, since it's not a threat but more of a bonus. As neuropsychologist Rick Hanson, the author of *Hardwiring Happiness*, told me when I interviewed him: "Miss a tiger today and you won't be around tomorrow. Miss a carrot today, and you'll have more chances to get one tomorrow." This describes how our nervous systems evolved to process data and information: we have an easy time focusing on what is negative just in case we need to learn something from it to help us survive! And the good stuff is often lost on us, unless we place our attention on it and intentionally help ourselves learn from what is good in our lives.

The negativity bias influences the coherent story loops in our heads. We have more negative stories than positive ones because we are tracking how things might go wrong and plotting our reaction if they do. It's more satisfying to our primitive brains to obsess about potential danger (*What will happen to my career, my future, if I flub this presentation?*) than to focus attention on what is pleasant (*I love the feeling of that cool breeze and late afternoon sun* or *What a cool opportunity, getting to speak in front of my entire company!*). We are creatures that like the security of patterns even if they keep us in unconscious negative loops. We tend to cognitively take the path of least resistance, even when the path of least resistance doesn't help us.

There's good news, though: once we make what is unconscious conscious, we can find where we are holding ourselves back in our thinking patterns, and learn how to create new stories that are more flexible and true to the moment. The stories we create and the hallucinations we inhabit are trying to serve a function: to help us survive, and thrive. It's just that some are outdated and unquestioned, and don't help us at all. Stories frame our lives with nuance and texture, and can be heartbreakingly beautiful and passionate, boring, destructive, or anywhere in between. So let's take a deeper look together at some of the underlying patterns that drive the formation and maintenance of our coherent stories. When we illuminate them and peer into how our subconscious mind works, we automatically free up space to think out of the box—with creativity and freshness. When we're not stuck in a loop, we are open to what is actually in front of us. We can bring a beginner's mind to the staircase we are descending in the dark as well as to the person standing in front of us at the café. We can trust what we do know while making space for what we don't. Spontaneous, authentic action that meets the moment as it actually is, rather than as we think it is or should be, comes when we are unburdened of our inaccurate (bless our hearts) ideas and beliefs.

Decision-Making and Worldview

Our stories cause us to make decisions based on how we view the world, and we follow intuitions without much questioning; for example, when we have an intuition or hunch not to hire someone we've interviewed. It *works* to move through life trusting our gut and well-deserved wisdom, supported by the stories we create—*except when it doesn't.* What if that person you just rejected was a perfect fit for the job, but you failed to hire them because of faulty assumptions fueled by an inaccurate flash judgment? Or they were a terrible fit for the job, but because of a lightning-fast first impression you hired them and ended up dealing with three years of drama, sweeping up after their messes and then finally letting them go?

We all know the impact of making a quick decision based on a gut feeling and a sense of certainty and then being surprised by what we missed in that first encounter. And the stakes can be even higher when we look at what else our blind spots can obscure. A while ago—and even now if you live in a remote area—there were dire consequences to having a blind spot that made you miss the tiger creeping up behind you. Obliterated from the gene pool just like that! Nowadays blind spots can be costly in a different way. What we miss might not get us eaten by a tiger, but it can drive the stress response, foster war or disease, and create disharmony in our relationships, all of which eventually *can* eject us from the gene pool. The stress our stories cause can make us sick, and the violence and bigotry war causes can end up in genocide and mass displacement of human groups. And it's all in the name of our brain's need for a narrative that drives us to do, believe, and feel things about other groups of people that are unnecessary, untrue, and quite harmful. Think about the events in Charlottesville, Virginia, in 2017: even though white supremacy is a fringe belief in the United States, just one white man holding a story about one race being superior to all others ran a car into a crowd, killing an innocent woman who was standing up for the rights of her brothers and sisters.

That's the extreme end, but let's look at more common ways our minds work for and against us. To stay safe, navigate life, and even thrive, we create quick and easy stories (fixed ideas) about ourselves and our world that support us in survival, in being happy, and in getting what we (think we) want. No problem there—as I mentioned, it works most of the time. Our biology supports this. But what if we slow the process down and take a second look?

Stories don't always steer us in the right direction. Having a coherent narrative about something, no matter what it is, from "I'm fat" to "Immigrants are taking all our jobs" to "Our company is the best and will never be beat," may all be easy on the brain, but are they true? We are generally accurate with our stories—at least enough to keep from bumping into walls while walking, to agree that a red light means stop, and to remember people's names and the capital of Nebraska. So we tend to think *all* our stories are true. This is important to understand. Questioning our ideas and assumptions is hard. That's why we dupe ourselves; we confirm our own ideas so quickly, based on the assumption that we are accurate, that we miss the chance to see whether we missed something. Our need to create coherent stories and have them feel believable (and hence unquestioned) leads us to form and protect blind spots.

Part of the reason we think our beliefs are true is that it's cognitively taxing to question our own thinking—the physiological process uses up that sweet resource called glucose in our brains![2] Let me explain.

Blood Sugar and Questioning Assumptions

Have you ever had a "low blood sugar" moment when your brain didn't seem to be working? There's a biological study that supports this experience. Researchers have discovered that blood glucose—the level of sugar circulating in our blood at any given time, which is the primary source of energy for the body's cells—is an important energy source of self-control, and that acts of self-control, such as regulating attention for cognitive tasks like *questioning your own ideas* (called cognitive effort), deplete relatively large amounts of glucose. It takes energy to think analytically, and that energy comes in the form of glucose! When we replenish glucose in our body (say, by eating a blueberry muffin), we suddenly do better at stuff like controlling attention, regulating emotions, and coping with stress.[3]

So here's the kicker when it comes to blind spots: when we confirm our beliefs and assumptions without giving them a second thought, we aren't using up as much glucose, and we feel an innate confidence in how we view the world. It's easy on us. We assume we are right because our lack of questioning our assumptions makes us assume so. *Is that not such a trip?* We are so convinced we're right (partly) because it depletes glucose stores to double-check the truth. Our brains evolved to support us by sending our ideas and assumptions into our unconscious so we can automatically trust our instinctual judgment (*Don't step in that quicksand again! Remember what happened last time!*). It's useful in many cases, but the way this mechanism works in the modern world can harm us if we don't pay attention.

Say you're busy doing something like trying to remember your shopping list at the grocery store. You unquestioningly confirm the quick impressions—your intuitions and opinions—you form while there because your judgment system is distracted, using up glucose to do the important task of not forgetting the ketchup, dish soap, and tea: three things that are hard to remember all at once. Who has time to question their flash judgment about the annoying woman walking in front of them into the store when they are trying to remember *that* grocery list? It's easier on your whole system to confirm your intuitions and biases because the resources you have available to question them are limited. So you think, *That woman is so annoying, so entitled. She cut me off without even noticing I was there first to get a cart. What a brat. Okay, where are the condiments?*

Just think of the last time you vehemently believed something that turned out to be untrue. *Oh, wait . . .* it's not that easy to remember, is it? *We're so good at trusting that we're rational!* Our minds confirm our ideas as if they are objectively true and we miss what is right in front of us even if it may be plain for others to see. We tend to be none the wiser, until we do something like fall in love with a jerk or someone else hires the best person in our business space because our first impression left us thinking they weren't the right fit. Not questioning our beliefs creates camouflage for our blind spots. There's a reason why one of the biggest areas of conflict in relationships is when both people are convinced they are right and invested in proving to the other they are wrong: when we're entrenched in our point of view it's hard to see from another's.

Fast and Slow Thinking

Of course, the capacity to be reflective and flexible in our thinking is about more than blood sugar levels. In his book *Thinking, Fast and Slow*, psychologist and cognitive behaviorist Daniel Kahneman writes that we have two systems for processing information and making decisions: the "fast thinking" system works automatically and quickly, with little or no effort, and is involuntary; the "slow thinking" system usually confirms (and sometimes questions) the beliefs and choices of the fast-thinking system.[4]

These are generalizations—we don't have two separate mechanisms in our brains—but I like how Kahneman frames our thinking because he paints a clear picture of what happens unconsciously as we navigate the world, making choices and forming stories (and blind spots) along the way. When we use *fast thinking*, we tend to have glucose-saving *cognitive ease*—the assumptions and intuitions are automatic and effortless: *I don't like that guy.* If a belief feels familiar, true, right, and accessible, perhaps because we've thought it before or it just *seems* clear and rational, we are more likely to confirm that it is true, like declaring, "My company is the best in the space," instead of questioning it. It's easy on our brains.

Just as our fast-thinking system jumps to conclusions and creates coherent stories about what is going on around and inside of us, the *slow-thinking* system questions things. Slow thinking is a more deliberate way of thinking that requires attention and effort, is analytical and logical, and can exert self-control over the impulses of our fast-thinking system, such as *Wait a minute! There are three other companies listed ahead of mine in the app store, and five more that are approaching the success of my company. I guess we aren't the best in the space, but we're good enough and that's the story I'm going to present to my investors. Also, maybe I should stop badmouthing that other startup—they must be doing something right.* Or *I am turned off by that woman's behavior in the grocery store but maybe I'm just catching her in a bad moment, or maybe I'm the one feeling entitled!*

The strange thing in terms of blind spots is that our fast thinking creates them, but our slow thinking *often confirms them* without any reflective thinking. Doesn't that seem counterintuitive, when the slow-thinking system is built to be analytical and objective? Consider the times you've reflected thoughtfully as you judge the character of a person on a first date: Do they seem trustworthy? Did it feel authentic or forced when they leaned in to kiss you? The slow-thinking system *can* be used to question our choices, impulses, and intuitions, but it doesn't always do so; it's *more likely* to thoughtlessly confirm our fast-thinking choices and impulses (*I have to see her again!*) because (remember . . .) it takes energy to question our beliefs. We make lightning-fast judgments about the information our bodies and environments give us in every moment, and our slow thinking is a bit lazy in that it is selective about when it's used, especially when our quick impressions feel so right-on.[5]

We can, however, use our slow-thinking systems to do things like build skyscrapers and inquire into the nature of a belief, and when we think about it that way, it's amazing that we can learn how and what to consciously pay attention to, and what not to. It shows that, even though there's so much we miss, we are quite sophisticated in our ability to learn and apply knowledge and wisdom in our lives. It's just a matter of figuring out how to harness this capability! Discerning the filters that help us unwittingly believe our own ideas makes it easier to catch where we are blind. In doing so, we learn how to learn better.

Story Coherence

The measure of success for fast thinking, in terms of our ideas and beliefs getting confirmed without question, is the *coherence of the story*. Who has time to analyze every single thought that runs through her brain just to see if it is correct? If it seems true, it must be true, right? But the fact that it's coherent doesn't mean it's true. This is why mindfulness and other self-inquiry practices like journal writing and therapy are so important. When we slow down, we get in touch with specific beliefs and assumptions (stories and hallucinations!) that may be fueling our behavior unnecessarily, and awaken to the blind spot effect that causes stress and affects our work and home life. We can only do this when we are willing to take the time to hang out with our experience.

We start to see how much we *don't* see and *don't* know, and that can be scary or liberating, or both. If you discover you are doing something from a blind spot that has caused all kinds of extra suffering just to support a coherent story—like, for instance, believing you're all alone in the world—and to sustain that story you push people away and consistently feel that no one understands you, do you think you might be willing to take a second look? Most of us would answer yes, yet it can be painful to let go of our ideas because we're so darn used to them and they've become part of who we are.

There's even something called the "endowment effect" that describes how we weight what we have now as more valuable than what we will gain if we give up what we have.[6] That goes for selling your house, but also for holding on to your beliefs and assumptions about your spouse, your child, your parent, and yourself. The antidote to the suffering our faulty stories creates is hidden within them: when we take the time to kindly question our ideas and assumptions, the truth is revealed and our blind spots come into the light. When we see clearly and let go of a coherent story that doesn't quite feel true anymore, we do gain something. It's just not always what we wanted it to be: we gain the truth, which isn't so easy to swallow sometimes, and asks us in facing it to take an action in our lives. The action may simply be telling ourselves the truth and allowing it to germinate, or it may be to have a conversation with someone or make a tough decision. In doing so we get to update our file and gain a more coherent story. We also remain open to continuing to learn and grow from what is right in front of us, because life is that generous and relentless. It keeps giving us situations where we are forced to choose: either stay entrenched in a belief and suffer, or open and grow.

PRACTICE Testing Story Coherence

Here's how to choose opening and growing! When you feel stuck in a situation or find yourself frustrated or in conflict with someone, you can use this quick-and-easy formula to check out your stories.

- Think of a scenario in which you are certain you are right, one where your holding that belief has an energetic charge to it, such as "My boss is stupid" or "My partner isn't there for me." Let's say you keep seeing proof that your ideas are true: your boss makes a careless mistake during a presentation or your partner forgets to pick you up at the airport. This is how we build coherent stories, and stress ourselves (and others) out when they loop around in our heads.

- To interrupt that pattern, ask, "Is there anything about this thought that I'm believing because it's an easy, coherent story? Is there more to the story than this? What is at stake for me right now?"

You might be surprised at what comes to you if you inquire in this way. You know deep down what is most true, and you can trust that it will come into the light if you give it space and a bit of presence. Things gain nuance and texture when you start to see the whole picture and mindfully question your ideas and assumptions. We like to think we have the whole story, and when we do it makes us feel good (and justified) in our understanding of any given situation. It's so natural to do this! We learn from our environment, and when we can safely say that a staircase is a staircase, we don't have to pause before stepping out toward an unknown descent, wondering if that next step will be there for us.

Having a belief or point of view is similar. We're asserting its trustworthiness: "I know this to be true!" Yet we are really saying, "This is what I know *so far*." For those of us who like to have control or be the on-scene expert, that's a hard thing to admit.

Often, our belief seems partly true—"My boss is *a bit* stupid"—but we can also start to take into account what we aren't seeing, which makes it easier to see from someone else's perspective. "My boss gives me the feeling that he's stupid when he talks to me that way. I don't think he's listening, though. Since I get the impression he doesn't understand, I'm going to ask him if I can be clearer with my requests, and I'm going to try to catch him at times when he isn't distracted." When we see that we hold only part of the story, we can open to creative opportunities. This also helps us be open to being disproved, and willing to rewrite the story. Our stories aren't always wrong, but holding our fixed ideas more loosely helps us see what is most true, to the best of our ability in any given situation. And it helps to understand what is at stake for us when we are believing a thought, like *My partner isn't there for me.* Perhaps we come to see that we need support and are feeling hurt because it wasn't given in a way that we needed it. When we get in touch with what is really there, we can share from our vulnerability rather than blame, and that can be a game-changer in relationships.

Another way to view this is that, while applying our insightful, slow-thinking system to question our stories uses up our glucose resources (and our time), it's worth it. The amount of energy that gets freed up when we see clearly relieves our suffering, and then it becomes a natural reflex to pause and question. That's when we start loving the journey of discovery.

Practice and Insight

Is there a way to hack our mind's faulty assumptions, stop spending so much effort dealing with the suffering they create, and instead use the way we are wired to learn to up-level our lives and release ourselves from unnecessary suffering? (Just think of all the drama we cause in relationships as a result of the fixed ideas about the other person—which we don't even see—that form a lens through which we see them.)

Our slow-thinking system, which is analytical and reflective, can be enlisted to help us move the default setting in our fast-thinking system from an unquestioned negativity bias to a questioning and open mind, contributing to an overall sense of well-being and ease. We can also use our slow-thinking system in a skillful way to migrate mindful behaviors—such as being compassionate and kind instead of reactive and impulsive—to the fast-thinking system so they too become automatic and effortless, and free up attention to illuminate our blind spots.

Let me give you an example. When we learn to drive, we are employing slow thinking as we focus attention on the wheel, the road, and the feeling of the brake underneath our foot. Driving a car demands a lot of effort at first, and you may even feel exhausted from the focus and control you have to exert. Fast-forward five years later, and driving has become automatic (fast thinking) and you no longer need such concentrated effort. The same can be said about learning to tie your shoes, speak Spanish, or be mindful. It takes time and effort to learn something new.

To hack our thinking system to make wise, compassionate behaviors effortless, we employ the two key mechanisms of mindfulness: *practice* and *insight*. By *practice*, I mean training your attention through a mindfulness exercise, such as resting your attention gently on the breath flowing in and out, letting go of distractions, and paying attention to what is in your present-moment experience. By *insight*, I mean seeing deeply and clearly into the nature of your experience, finding the underlying cause of a feeling or situation, and coming up with innovative ways to deal with that cause. Insight can be used to ask any question you hold about yourself, others, or the world around you.

Practice and insight can work in tandem or separately. Practice works, over time if you do it regularly, to shift behaviors—toward, for example, responding to challenging situations with curiosity and kindness—from effortful to automatic. Insight works in a moment of clear seeing that helps you get to the core of the matter, freeing your behavior to match what you know internally, hence making it automatic and effortless. Practice and insight both need slow thinking at first; i.e., pausing to take several mindful breaths or questioning your beliefs and assumptions. Yet pausing to take a breath or to see *can* become automatic and effortless, taking place outside of your conscious awareness and forceful self-control, with a feeling of naturalness and ease. With the application of practice and insight, there's a rewiring of your brain: you shift from your default negativity bias, with its fixed ideas, to a different kind of default setting that is open and curious without being unnatural or forced.

TRIGGER FINGER

Let's look at an example of how this idea might be put to use in the workplace. Say you have a habit of firing off angry emails or texts to your colleagues (you just can't help yourself!). Using your slow-thinking hack, you could practice mindfully slowing down and pausing, asking, *Do I need to send this right now? Can it wait an hour, or a day?* Stopping to reflect before you hit "send" (slow thinking) can be energetically taxing at first because in some ways it's just easier—instant gratification—to press "send." We have all been there: it can feel so right to press that button, can't it? It temporarily relieves us of the misery of being with our experience! It's like tossing an emotional hot potato, in the form of words and emojis, to someone else. If you persist in practicing a pause before pressing "send," however, your habitual reactive way of being will gradually change because you will *learn that it's beneficial to wait*—and now *that* becomes automatic. Eventually you don't need to exert brain power in the form of blood glucose and self-control to refrain from sending that email, and the pause becomes effortless.

That's the practice part of using slow thinking to hack a behavior over time. Now comes insight. It's the quick hack of our fast- and slow-thinking systems. If we *see through* a belief that is limiting us in some way—a coherent story we are holding that is untrue—and a blind spot is revealed, we can perform a fast hack of our thinking system. Let's go back to those work emails. Say one day you're sitting at your desk reflecting on the stress of your office interactions, and it occurs to you that there may be something you're not seeing about this email situation that has become such a habit of tension and impulsivity. Your stance is open and undefended, and you are curious about what is going on. This is a fertile moment. Encountering what you don't know can even have a poetic quality to it, as you hazily see the core of the pattern but don't yet quite see it fully; it's like a work of art coming into focus. As you stare, daydreaming, at the calendar on your cubicle wall, it hits you that you've been hurting *yourself* by sending these emails, and that nobody else is doing that hurtful thing *to* you. You're not a victim in this. Your reaction to the ignorance and incompetence of those around you has seemed so righteous, but then, with insight, like an accountant, you start to tally the time you spend cleaning up the messes your own hasty communications make and you see the issue—a blind spot comes into view. You realize that even though you've been blaming your colleagues, it's *your* behavior of firing off these impetuous emails in response that has been causing you (not to mention others around you) to suffer. Yes, there's your blind spot!

There's a fine line between feeling like a victim and taking responsibility for your own participation in a dynamic. Sometimes people treat you badly and you need to create boundaries and make requests, or end relationships or jobs because of difficult relational conditions, and it sucks. But seeing through the story of being a victim—a person trapped by someone else's behavior—is vital if you are to see your blind spots and learn how to learn better. This is key in stopping the cycle of suffering and gaining empowerment and agency. If you released being victimized, caught in the trap of the behavior of someone who has hurt you, what would that look like in real time, in real life?

The Fast Hack of Taking Responsibility

In the situation where you've been firing off impetuous emails and have seen with insight into your blind spot, you are now 100 percent convinced that your patterned behavior is unhelpful and doesn't produce the desired response, so you stop sending those types of messages. You see that even though you've been feeling like a victim of your colleagues and your responses felt justified, you've been participating in a dynamic that is not bringing clarity or resolution to the issues at hand. You recognize that it's not kind to others, but it's also not kind to you. It's like you don't have a choice anymore—it's that clear. *You now see your part in the cycle.* Eventually, the impulse to react in that way stops arising altogether.

Now you have a kinder, more reflective way of operating, via your fast-thinking (automatic) system, and it's cognitively easy and feels good and right because it *is* right. Your coherent story gets a little more real and a little more coherent. You move closer to the truth of things. You don't have to use up a bunch of precious glucose to slow yourself down, pause, and reflect before sending an email. You've cut through your own bullshit and shone a light on a blind spot—namely being reactive and blaming others and trying to get other people to change so *you* can be happy, all the while thinking you are righteous, blameless, and a victim of their behavior. *Doesn't it feel good to let all that go?*

This frees you to explore the underlying issues. Your clear perception brings insight and allows for all kinds of creative and compassionate responses to tricky scenarios. By not making other people wrong, you can take responsibility when it's yours to take, and make clear requests of your colleagues or managers without feeling like a victim of their behavior. You now have choice. When you reflect, backtracking to that point where you had felt wronged and impulsively reacted over email, you can see where you went blind to yourself and make a commitment to catch this in the future and honor your feelings. Your blind spot has helped you get in touch with your own autonomy and empowerment: What a revolutionary idea!

●

Both ways of approaching this issue—practicing over time to pause and reflect before pressing "send," and suddenly having a deep, clear insight into your blind spot behavior—take you to the same place. Both practice and insight help you shift kind and wise behavior from slow to fast thinking, where it becomes automatic and effortless. As I mentioned earlier, they often work in tandem. Rather than having your automatic behavior skew toward reactivity, anger, or anxiety, you can help other responses such as compassion and understanding become instinctual, and lightning fast. That's the up-leveling.

Paradox Alert: Letting Go, and Taking Responsibility

If we want to see all the way into our blind spots, it comes down to being willing to let go of control and fixed ideas: seeing the brick wall as immovable and the rocks as un-stackable. In this way we let wisdom, insight, and relaxation in and navigate life according to more essential and aligned truths. Both paths support us as we drop the inner (and outer) struggle, yet sometimes we need to struggle before letting go and receiving sight and, ultimately, insight. This can happen slowly or in a flash, and it helps us in not only seeing the elephant in the room but in knowing what to do with the fact that it's there. This kind of truthfulness lets us access our body's natural wisdom. We already know just what to do and we can trust that. It's when we cover up our knowing and seeing that we get into trouble.

It's scary to be in touch with what is unknown or unfamiliar, and it's scary to debunk a belief about someone we don't like. It's also threatening to take responsibility for our half of the equation because we're afraid doing so will be misconstrued as admitting we did something wrong. I wonder if we aren't all, at our core, scared of receiving blame, of being wrong—so we blame others (or ourselves) before anyone else has a chance to do it. It's uncomfortable navigating a situation without the "benefit" of our preconceived notions and fixed ideas, but it's so much more alive and real when we do, isn't it? In relaxing our tightly held opinions, we start to see more points of view, and creative solutions arise from our inner wisdom.

Although it's counterintuitive, claiming responsibility for our part is actually a relief; it empowers rather than disempowers. When our choices come from this kind of clear seeing, they can be proactive and responsive in any given moment. This way of being helps us explore a horizon of experience that we can't quite see past. But when we get the hang of it, we realize that we are more intelligent when we spend time welcoming what is unknown to us. It enables us to see what is really there and no longer see what is *not* there. Then we can claim what we now know with humility, clarity, and conviction.

Feeling comfortable with the unknown while being in touch with what we *do* know deep down, rather than insisting we know and are right (my way or the highway), can become our new default setting. The actions that come from this new way of being may surprise us but they feel more aligned to the situation and what the moment calls for. What we don't know and don't see has gifts hidden within, if we take the time to look. We gain clarity when we face the unknown, and mindfulness supports that. That's why we usually need both paths to grow in a balanced and stable way: the insight path can bring us huge leaps in understanding, while the practice path helps us integrate them into our lives.

Moving the Arrow on Your Default State—Toward Flow

Remember the Five Mindful Breaths practice we did in chapter 1? When we first learn this practice, it takes effort to place attention on the breath, or another focus point, as we train our minds to relax and notice thoughts as they come and go without getting involved in them, all while resting naturally with presence to what arises.

Stop for a minute now and take a few mindful breaths, and see how you feel as you do so.

With practice, these attentional focus activities will become second nature—they won't take much effort at all. Your *default* attentional setting will become more present, easeful, and content. You will be able to see what happens in a way you couldn't before, and have access to choices and responses rather than to victimhood and reactivity. By doing this simple practice again and again, you are steadily moving the arrow from blindness to a default state called "flow."

It is said that the flow state is complete absorption in the task at hand without any reflective self-consciousness or exertion of self-control, with time and space falling away, and action and awareness merging.[7] Meditation states have a similar definition, referring to subject and object merging, or "action and awareness" no longer being separate.

Blind spots operate unconsciously and automatically while flow operates *consciously* and automatically. The state of blindness comes from being lost and not seeing clearly, while the state of flow comes from being found and letting go from a place of clear seeing.

Flow was what the long-term meditators experienced when they caught the data in the attentional blink study that the novice meditators missed. With more cognitive ease and availability of attention, they had more energy to spot what was right in front of them. This is also what fMRI (functional magnetic resonance imaging which non-invasively measures brain activity) scans measuring people's brains in meditation show: newbies tend to use their prefrontal cortex (the area associated with cognitive processes and decision-making) to exert effort to concentrate, while advanced practitioners don't activate that same place in their brain. There is much less self-control and effort in the latter scenario, which is why many meditators experience effortlessness and ease in concentration.[8]

Whatever path you take to get to flow and conscious, clear seeing, when you use that state to illuminate the blind spots in your thinking, it can be radical and transformative. It's a little bit like Einstein having an insight that changes everything in the seeing of it. By making one big discovery, we find that everything else looks different. Even if we are just discovering a thought about ourselves that was false, that didn't hold up under the light, sometimes that discovery is the underpinning of a whole way of viewing our world. This is why looking at blind spots takes courage. If the discovery is penetrating enough and clear enough, it can hack our wiring to help us see past and through the brick wall in front of us and reveal options we never saw before. If we see that a certain behavior or belief is working against us and causing unnecessary stress and harm, that insight can free our attention to learn something new. What fixed idea are you holding that you could question? Where would those questions lead?

Binge-Watching and Blind Spots

Have you ever been really good at exerting self-control for a period of time—over your diet, say, or what you take in digitally—and then . . .

suddenly find yourself binge-eating a pint of ice cream or a bag of chips, or binge-watching a Netflix series, or binge-scrolling through Facebook or Twitter? Ironically, *exerting* self-control leads to the depletion of our precious brain resources, powered by glucose, and hence the *depletion* of self-control! At some point, we give up, and give in. The name for the exertion of will or self-control is called *ego depletion*.[9] How apt! When we understand that we can get depleted when we exert self-control, we have another way to look at blind spots.

Consider the head-in-the-sand metaphor: it's less depleting (at least in the short term) to block out what we don't want to deal with, even if it is causing us a ginormous amount of trouble, like adding a few pounds in the form of ice cream and cookies. Think of a time you ignored what you knew was best because it felt easier, or you made a behavior change and then fell back into the old pattern—that is the power of a default setting! It takes effort to create a new default, as we have seen. In this kind of situation, our blindness takes the form of laziness and habit.

Matthew Gailliot and Roy Baumeister, two social psychologists at Florida State University, have performed research suggesting that suppressing our natural tendencies (by exerting self-control) takes a ton of effort in the form of mental exertion. It's why after a few tries at keeping ourselves from that second piece of chocolate cake, our final response might be, "Oh well, fuck it!" and we just eat the cake. We need glucose anyway, right? And guess what researchers found. *It works the same way with intuitions and decisions.*[10] As we have seen, we end up *not* exerting the effort to check our first impressions or intuitions, because our slow-thinking system is energetically "lazy."

And that has an impact on all kinds of things, such as hiring the wrong person because you didn't listen to the hunch that told you to slow it down and take time to interview more candidates. Intuitive errors are more common when we are depleted from suppressing our tendencies (being self-controlled). Sound familiar? Just as it's easier and less energetically taxing to eat the piece of cake than to not eat it, or to spend two hours mindlessly scrolling through Facebook than not scrolling through Facebook. All of this takes place subconsciously, of course. Is it possible to have self-control but not let it take so much energy from our body's resources? What would that even look like?

A Self-Control Hack

It's the *ability to not be tempted or distracted by these urges at all that separates those with mastery from the rest of us!* When we see our blind spots, we have the capacity to see all the way through. People with mastery hack the code to the core of the blind spot itself.

Let's bring this idea down to earth a little. Nowhere does our clear seeing go more cloudy than when we're in a moment of conflict. Let's say you always fight with your dad about finances, even though you haven't lived at home in fifteen years. The subject of money brings up strong emotions for both of you, and you always end up feeling wounded, upset, and misunderstood. You know better than to do this dance again, and so does he, but you can't help yourselves. You keep falling into the pattern, like when you mindlessly binge-scroll through Facebook.

For a self-control hack, you could see all the way through your story, noticing the complex emotions that arise and understanding that the subject is a minefield that is hard to traverse. If you get to the core—which, you discover through your hacking, is the fact that you wish your dad was different from who he is (and he hasn't changed in the thirty-five years you have known him)—by understanding your point of view and no longer judging *you*, you are approaching insight. Herein, in your wish that your dad was different, lies your suffering—it's not the actual conflict at all!

Now, what if you didn't pick up the emotional hot potato that is this repetitive dynamic, and instead did something else without giving up your voice and position? What might that be? When you do this, you begin to see your deeper underlying feelings and become more kind to yourself, knowing your triggers and letting go of the need to assert your truth. Instead you can rest in that truth without needing another person (in this case, your dad) to accept it.

All sorts of creative options arise when you look to the core of an issue—that was just one possible discovery. It may dawn on you instead that you have been judging *yourself* about money and your father's judgment highlights where you are holding a belief about how you should be with money. So you can thank him! He's helping you see more clearly. Eventually, the urge to engage your dad on this issue may not tempt or distract you at all: that is the hack. You see through it before it becomes a real thought.

I understand that it's not *easy* to get to the core of things but the core is usually *simple* when we do. It becomes easier to not engage in the conflict if you've let go of your self-judgment and feel okay with his judgment. Who knows—maybe you're judging the heck out of him for being hypercritical when all he wants is to feel heard!

PRACTICE **The Conflict Urge Hack**

The next time you just cannot seem to resist a conflict that constantly repeats itself in a pattern, try asking yourself:

How do I wish the other person would be right now?

Maybe you wish they would see your point of view and stop being so stuck in their own. Or you wish they would stop judging you. Or you wish they would just take a moment and empathize with how you're feeling.

Now give that same thing to yourself.

See your own point of view. See theirs. Stop judging them and stop judging yourself. Empathize with how you're feeling right now, and how they might be feeling. Then come back to the conflict and see what happens.

Do you have a different request of them, and a different frame for approaching your discussion? Let's say you're in a big picture/small picture conflict. You want you and your partner to focus on the macro and she wants to dig into the micro of some situation. Perhaps you say something like, "You know, I bet you experience my need to not get bogged down with the details as chaotic, and I experience your need for answers as controlling. Is that your experience? How can we come to a place of shared understanding here, or is there a good way to meet each other in the middle? Or do you think we should just pause the discussion for now and circle back later?"

This example of conflict is powerful because this kind of dynamic is a part of everyone's lives, and one that is rife with blind spots. When we keep getting pulled back into a conflict, it takes effort to untangle ourselves and avoid getting caught up in it, doesn't it? No harm there; we all do that innocently enough, and we do our best. Conflict is tough. If we can see all the way through the nature of a conflict, to its core, however, the urge to get pulled in isn't as strong. We have given up trying to change someone else and understood what our own needs are and are still able to make clear requests, set boundaries, and be compassionate because we see from a more holistic view. When we reach that stage, that is some serious up-leveling in our navigation through life, and it takes some real work to get there as we learn to navigate the unique landscape of each personal relationship. When a behavior is no longer interesting or tempting to us because *we know it doesn't work* and it hurts us, and we understand its essence and admit to ourselves what is going on without resisting it, that's when we've reached a level of automaticity in self-control (or the ability to effortlessly not pick up what someone just put down in front of us because we see the consequences, and now it's uninteresting and doesn't even trigger us). Gaining this level of freedom doesn't mean, however, that we have to tolerate an untenable situation.

Blame, making the other person wrong, and defending a stance aren't useful, even though they have the pull and believability of their own story. Taking responsibility, taking leadership, seeing the situation and the person for how they are rather than how you want them to be, setting boundaries, welcoming our own challenging emotions, and making clear requests *are* useful. And it's likely that the story that goes along with those actions is more coherent and closer to what is true, and will bring ease to the conflict rather than entangling you in it. This is why insight is so valuable. Just telling yourself to be a certain way will only get you so far—like telling yourself to pause before sending that text. Seeing through the pattern and blind spot will interrupt the impulse to send it!

Something in It for You

If I'm in a conflict and am defending an image of myself, there is something in it for me and a lot is at stake. But if I'm undefended yet compassionate, and truthful with clear boundaries, there isn't anything in it for *the me that is my idealized self-image*. And ironically, I get a lot more out of the interaction when I approach it in this way, with vulnerability and clarity. Only when we have hacked all the way through it and gleaned insight about why a behavior isn't working and hurts us do we become free. Conflict is hard; we get angry and hurt, and it's natural and normal to do so. Getting insight into our stuck places doesn't make us free *from* our challenging feelings and hurt places; it makes us free *to* feel and experience what is really there, and mindful practices like self-kindness support us as we journey through the relational terrain of our lives.

We can't force insight and clear seeing. It has its own unfolding, and we can't leap past where we are right now. Or so I've noticed. The poet Rainer Maria Rilke wrote, "May what I do flow like a river, no pushing and no holding back, the way it is with children."[11] When we see and let go in this way, our attention is freer; we can see from a 360-degree view without it feeling cumbersome. We *see more* but are *less burdened*. And we are no longer trying to control the heck out of everything, which leaves room for a little more wonder and creativity. We can turn something as simple as stacking rocks into a feat of physics and martial arts moves into creek-bed magic.

•

As we close this chapter, let's get a little practice working with its main theme: coherent stories.

PRACTICE   Questioning "Coherent" Stories

Think of a belief you're holding that forms a coherent story. It could be about yourself or about someone else. Then ask yourself these three questions:

    1 *What is my belief here?*

    2 *Is there more to the story than this? If I weren't holding this to be true, what statement would be more true?*

    3 *Is there an action I can take now that I have a more coherent story?*

Here's an example to get you started: 1. *My girlfriend doesn't support me.* 2. *My girlfriend is supportive generally but sometimes she lets me down.* 3. *I'm going to thank her for being supportive and explain how she can be even more so in certain situations.*

There's much more to explore about how our minds work to create and maintain blind spots, and how we can interrupt those patterns. In chapter 3 we'll continue our discussion about fast thinking and take a look at mental shortcuts, intuition, and the state of flow.

3

SHORTCUT TO FLOW STATE
Hacking Faulty Intuitions

It is how we choose what we do, and how we approach it,
that will determine whether the sum of our days adds up to
a formless blur, or to something resembling a work of art.
MIHALY CSIKSZENTMIHALYI[1]

MARIO GALARRETA, a cellular neuroscientist, neurologist, and
filmmaker who works on the Wellbeing team at Google, told me a
compelling story about the blind spot of stillness. He and I co-taught
the Search Inside Yourself program at Google, and later worked on
a project breaking down the science of what happens in the brain
during mindfulness practice into understandable language for facilita-
tor trainees in the program's training institute. We love meeting up
and geeking out about scientific inquiry and meditation. As we riffed
about blind spots, he exclaimed, "We thought for so many centuries
that *we* were still, and *the sun* was revolving around us. We were sitting
here on Earth in our little chairs," he said, grasping the sides of his
chair and gazing at the ceiling, "in utter stillness looking up at the sky,
convinced our world was not moving. How could it be? We believed
the sun was moving and we weren't and we didn't question it!" He
looked at me excitedly. "And to think at what speed we are spinning
on an axis, and simultaneously orbiting the sun, is incredible. It took
centuries to reveal this blind spot of stillness!"

Funny how the simple act of being curious—the basic quality of
everyone from an infant to a many-degreed research scientist—has

led to innovative leaps in our understanding of matter and energy and dramatically shifted our shared worldview. As Confucius apparently said: "To know that we know what we know, and to know that we do not know what we do not know, that is true knowledge."[2] The search for blind spots is the same: the simple act of being curious about the edge of our own understanding while questioning implicit assumptions can shift us into a state of flow, as opposed to living confined by the hardened ideas that limit our view of the world.

Fast Thinking, Mental Shortcuts, and Flow

We can use meditation to help us enhance our curiosity in the face of the unknown as part of our instinctual response to the vicissitudes of life. What if your default setting was curious instead of reactive? And even if you had a reaction, you were fundamentally curious about it and about what is most true? Rather than seeing what is not known to us as threatening (Galileo was placed under house arrest for agreeing with Copernicus that the Earth orbited the sun and not the other way around), we can see what is not known to us as an invitation into a dialogue at the border of what we are learning. This is akin to an open state of flow where we aren't clinging to our ideas that obfuscate life but are surfing the unknown naturally, updating our navigation system moment by moment.

Our fast-thinking mode is designed to systematize our lives and help guide us like a GPS to make lightning-fast intuitions and judgments, and we can harness it to help us stay on track with the useful qualities of openness and curiosity. Yet our quick thinking can sometimes be wrong, as when we make an assumption that the planet we inhabit doesn't move at all.

What's stopping us from living all the moments—good and bad, seen and unseen—with this quality of flow in and presence to our own lives? How do we learn the art of letting go, of not needing to hold on, without losing touch with our center and our deeper knowing? We understand that our blind spots are created through our unwillingness to question the fixed ideas and assumptions that we hold about ourselves, others, and the world around us. Some of the biggest blind spots blocking our participation in flow, however, are created and supported by the tiniest and most innocent of biases and moments, combining to form ideas and stories that keep confirming themselves and feeling believable.

Mental shortcuts are just such things. They are lightning-quick intuitive judgments that are common to all of us. They often work, but when they don't, they lead to cognitive biases that obscure our seeing. These can take many forms, three of which I'll highlight here:

1 Believing ideas because they are readily available to us: *availability* bias

2 Finding data that confirms what we already believe: *confirmation* bias

3 Thinking we saw things coming when we didn't, which makes us think we are better at predicting the future than we are: *hindsight* bias[3]

Mental shortcuts like these help us simplify things as we navigate the complexities and unknowns of life. But they hinder us when they cause us to gloss over or misperceive complexities that might actually require our attention, and that's bound to go wrong sometimes.

When do mental shortcuts interfere with our ability to experience flow and mindful awareness throughout our day? When do they back up untrue stories about ourselves or the world around us? Can seeing how our biases help us filter the world also help us see where we may have hidden blind spots?

Unconscious Traps

To answer these questions, one of the best things we can do is pull back the curtain on our unconscious operating systems. Once we've seen the inner workings of those systems—examining how we organize and filter information—we are far more likely to catch ourselves when we're falling into our own innocent little traps. Daniel Kahneman and his colleague Amos Tversky developed some groundbreaking insights into human judgment as it applies to behavioral economics: namely, that people who make decisions and form judgments under uncertainty make systematic mistakes that are common to all humans.[4] Their findings have brought into question the long-held assumption of human rationality, and have had broad impacts across diverse domains, bringing to light ways our cognitive biases cause us to make errors in judgments and decision-making. As we have discovered, we humans tend to think we are rational most of the time. *It's that exact blind spot that is most in our way.*

Kahneman and Tversky's work is still some of the most often cited in social science, and has been used with great success in the fields of medical diagnosis, intelligence analysis, philosophy, finance, statistics, and military strategy. Even though we *are* rational and can be right-on in our judgments and decisions, they poked holes in the image we hold about ourselves that we are *often* rational and right, and showed that the errors we make are common and applicable to everyone, experts included. The fact that they are considered rock stars in the world of behavioral economics shows how relevant their findings are across fields of study. We like to discover patterns of errors so we can course-correct! This helps the bottom line in businesses and government, but also has implications for relationships at home and work.

One significant thread that runs through all the biases they describe goes back to what we covered earlier, story creation: specifically, trying to create a *coherent* story from what we see so that the onslaught of information we receive each day doesn't confuse our brains—whether we're accessing a false memory of the past or assuming that an idea is accurate because it's similar to something else that is unrelated. It's precisely the creation of a coherent story that keeps us from questioning what we assume to be true.[5]

Hacking Biases

Let's look at the remarkable world of our mind's coherence-creating habits, and how and when we are likely to be fooled by those habits—for example, anyone who has ever looked up at the sun, seen it "rise and set," and made an assumption that the sun was orbiting the Earth and not the other way around. The awesome thing is that once we start to see how much of our experience is driven by unconscious biases, we can learn to look up at the sun as Copernicus did and experience a moment of insight and discovery; we can flip the orbit and change our world.

Take, for example, a fixed view you have about your coworker: that person is *lazy, uncaring, selfish*. Would you want someone to hold a fixed and unquestioned assumption like that about you? "Oh, she was like that ten years ago—I'm sure she's still the same." Or let's say you have a preconceived idea about who your ideal partner is, so you miss the love of your life, someone who has been standing right in front of you for seven years. Not to mention all the fixed ideas and beliefs you hold about *yourself*.

Not only can we limit ourselves when we miss the good stuff, but we can also feel held captive by our own and others' negative views of us. Let's dive into the three cognitive biases Kahneman and Tversky researched, to up-level our inner and outer relationships and the way we piece the world together. By understanding how we *systematically go blind*, we can investigate the nature of our fixed beliefs and positions and experience life from new, creative angles. While Kahneman and Tversky were looking at how these biases contributed to errors in decision-making, I'm looking at how they help us create blind spots in our worldview.

MENTAL SHORTCUT #1   AVAILABILITY BIAS

We predict outcomes and confirm our intuitions based on the ease of availability of information. Information enters our minds from all sorts of sources: our salient emotional memories; our exposure to data, facts, and opinions of any sort, including what we read and hear through the media and the internet; even the content of what we were just thinking about. When information is easy to recall, we tend to affirm our intuitions about a decision or judgment we need to make. This shortcut helps us believe that if we can bring examples and scenarios readily to mind, they are likely to be reliable and true.[6]

Later we will look at how our powers of intuition help us, and find ways to align with what is true and reliable, but for now let's focus on how our intuition hinders us. Take Carrie, for instance. She is planning a vacation to Paris. Her biggest fear is the possibility of a terrorist attack. In the last few years she has seen terrorist attacks on the news, and is aware of the increasing violence in Europe and the rise of religious extremism. She feels sheepish about her concern but can't help but be scared that she might get caught up in a violent act, as tourist sites seem to be the primary targets. Because this readily available (the result of multiple exposures in the media) fearful assumption comes to her mind, it is a factor for her as she considers visiting Paris. Ultimately her fear spoils her dream vacation to the City of Light; she decides to stay at home where it's safer and take a road trip instead. Yet ironically, her likelihood of dying in a car wreck in the United States is exponentially higher than her odds of experiencing a terrorist attack in Paris. This effect of availability bias happened after September 11, 2001; the number of road trippers increased, leading to a higher number of road accidents.[7]

In making her vacation choice, Carrie conflates the ease with which this risk comes to her mind with how panicked it makes her feel and the likelihood it could happen to *her*. This is how we can go blind to statistics in the face of our intuitions and emotional pulls and triggers. Just think how this works on our political systems as well, driving the polarizing and fearful beliefs different parties hold about the world and each other. It is biases like these that can, at the extreme, cause violence and war. They form blind spots because they seem so believable.

Availability bias works in less obvious ways too, generating mental blind spots about ourselves and others we love. Imagine this: You're a female of normal healthy body weight, five-feet-five and 140 pounds, living in the United States. You are routinely bombarded with images that depict a small part of the population (tall, stick-thin, blonde, white models representing *a tiny percentage* of American women) selling everything from clothes to cars and presented as the ideal figure seemingly everywhere you look. Back in high school, all your friends dieted. Twenty years later, on a regular basis, you semiconsciously think several times a day that you need to lose weight because your thighs are too fat—because the thought is available to you, always right there, along with its emotional salience. Do you think that you will wake up one morning and slip into your blue jeans and the thought will suddenly become unbelievable? Put another way, will statistics matter? *Probably not.* And just how much suffering is this available thought causing in your life, subconsciously or not? You're comparing yourself with 5 percent of the population 100 percent of the time when in reality you are representative of the majority of those around you, and your comparison is based on a persistent image of beauty rather than what is in your actual, observable experience.

That is the availability bias at work, in this case blocking us from being in the flow and being comfortable in our own bodies. Because we return to the image and the thought again and again (negativity bias at work!), some part of our experience is preoccupied with trying to be different and hating ourselves. Can you see how much of our thinking is driven by ideas that, due to their availability and ease of recall, seem true? I've heard it said that most of our thoughts are recycled. It's not like we thought them up all on our own. They come in to us from our families, our cultures, and through our own minds, and we snatch them up as if they were true. How often do you find yourself thinking, and confirming, the same thought repeatedly?

PRACTICE   **Your Body Stories**

Here's a good exercise to try to work with blind spots around body image.

- Take a moment to reflect upon a belief that you have about your body or appearance that persists in the background, using up some level of unconscious attention and energy. Write it down, or just hold it in your mind.

In his research on availability bias Kahneman wrote, "The proof that you truly understand a pattern of behavior is that you know how to reverse it."[8] Consider that. When you see a pattern, you have

options and can tell yourself a different coherent story—one that is
more true and relevant and helpful to you in your life.

- Now ask, *What if I had never had that thought about myself?*
  What would I be telling myself instead? See if you can flip it,
  like Copernicus, and instantly change your inner world.

Incidentally, I don't think any individual is to blame for this self-
image phenomenon—certainly not a woman who battles that image. I
believe it's our collective neurosis, operating in an unfortunate histori-
cal and cultural context, that keeps this one going. But just think: you
could go through your life struggling against your thighs (no matter
how much you weigh, from stick thin to large and curvaceous) and
spending a good amount of time trying to be different, wishing you
looked like what you see in magazines, contracted and disempowered.
And then there you are at the end of your life with your ashes being
sprinkled into the ocean by your family—did your thighs ever matter?
How much of your time did you lose in worrying about something
that had no basis in reality? So the next time you catch yourself believing something that comes to mind with ease simply because you have
heard it many times, ask yourself: *Does the fact that this came to mind*
as a possibility or fact make it true, or good? Is there a statistic or fact that
will help me understand the mistakenness of this thinking pattern? What
new, empowering story do I want to tell myself instead?

MENTAL SHORTCUT #2   CONFIRMATION BIAS

How can two people come away from the same situation with two
completely opposite stories? We see this so often in divorce cases, for
example, or in disagreements at work. We tend to confirm our exist-
ing beliefs rather than looking for new ones that might displace what
we already think, and we hold tight to what we think we know. Two
people can have a conversation and, because of their differing perspec-
tives, pick out key elements of it that bolster their own side of the story.
This is the source of misunderstanding. It feels safe to be right, and
scary to engage someone else who has an opposing view of the same

situation. We don't like to let in new information that may interrupt our beliefs, especially when we have been hurt or feel something is at stake. It's easier on the brain—less taxing, less glucose. And the world feels simpler, safer, and more manageable.

Yet sometimes only one person *is* right, right?

I once taught a class in the Middle East with a colleague of mine, a funny and super smart psychology professor from the University of Buffalo named Catherine Cook-Cottone. At one point during the course we had a mix-up: she thought I had skipped a slide, so she stood up to teach the piece of content she was sure I had missed. I, on the other hand, thought we hadn't gotten to the slide yet and wasn't sure why she suddenly popped out of her chair to teach something we had agreed I was supposed to handle. We each thought the other had made a mistake. It was a case where there was only one objectively true answer (either I skipped the slide or she jumped up early) but when we circled back to that moment, we had different recollections of the same event! We were both so curious about how that could be and we both felt so *right* in our views.

We laughed when we came to the conclusion that it didn't matter who was right; the important thing was that we discovered why we had each behaved as we did, which brought great relief to us as a team that cared deeply about the success of our project, and eased what could have become a moment of conflict. We could have begun to develop beliefs about one another—*She's so flighty* or *She just needs to be in the spotlight*—and then started looking for confirmation of those beliefs, had we not addressed this simple misunderstanding and discovered the truth.

There are times, of course, when one person's perspective is objectively true and it matters. People who intentionally manipulate and lie don't get to have their truth be "right" just because it's their perspective, and luckily, the truth has a way of revealing itself. There are facts, but no such thing as "alternative" facts. I'm speaking here to those times when we *don't see things objectively* and are instead seeing through a lens that confirms a preexisting idea, which can lead to overconfidence in our beliefs and poor decision-making. This is what Catherine and I narrowly avoided by surfacing the truth.

Another quick example: Say your adolescent son walks into the room with his head down. You make the assumption that he has an attitude, and you peer at him over your computer and launch into a speech about why he needs to get outside and get some exercise: *It's bad for you to be in your room spending so much time alone on your Xbox.* You "know" the reason his head's down so you don't even pause to think that he might be sad or tired, or that he just got into a fight with his sister and needs someone to talk to.

Much of the time, we see what we want to see rather than what is there. The filter of confirmation bias is like a biased scientist who is only interested in proving her hypothesis, not in discovering what's there. This filter is so strong, and so compelling, and we can be wholly blind to it. Try this the next time you face a decision where you feel sure about something, or when you have a different story or opinion from someone else. Ask yourself the following questions: *Just because this seems correct to me based on other information I have, does that mean it's true? Am I framing a question to get a certain response that I think might be true? Am I confirming an idea I have in order to manage this situation?* Allowing some ambiguity makes room for what you don't see accurately, and that's only going to help you become more compassionate and wise. And feel free to be right too. Here, we are just highlighting what happens when that mechanism goes wrong.

MENTAL SHORTCUT #3   HINDSIGHT BIAS

A veteran I met when I taught in San Quentin State Prison was the sole survivor of an ambush that occurred during a hostage rescue mission while he was in the US Special Forces. He shared that he continually runs scenarios in his mind about the traumatic incident, and feels convinced he could have prevented those deaths, despite the fact that there was no realistic possibility for him to handle that situation differently. He knows it's not true that he could have altered the outcome, but can't help going over and over the scenario in his head. This has led to a tremendous amount of guilt and anxiety, along with a suicide attempt while in prison. It's been working with his thought patterns through mindfulness and yoga that has given him relief from being trapped by this thinking bias. Thinking something was predictable in *hindsight* contributes to blind spots. It feeds regret—we wish we could turn the clock back and act differently—and our regret is based on the idea that we *could have*.[9] It's hard to admit *I didn't see it coming. I did the best I knew how in that moment, even though my best wasn't what it would be now, and if I knew what I know now I would do it differently.*

This fallacy also contributes to hindsight bias, making us think that the future is predictable: we believe we have figured out the past, which implies that the future should also be knowable. But in reality, we understand the past less than we think we do. The *illusion* that we understand the past feeds the *further illusion* that we can predict and control the future.[10] It's a nice idea: *reality is predictable*. But reality is far more ambiguous than we like to think. We use this hindsight filter to support a coherent story and to bolster our assumption that we understand much more than we do.

The next time you reflect on something that happened in the past and think you saw it coming, ask yourself: *Just because I think I saw this coming, does that make it true that I did? And does that make me a savvy predictor of what might happen next?* Seeing through this illusion can provide immense freedom for someone like the suffering veteran. Taking just a few moments to open to a far wider realm of possibility brings creativity and life to any situation. Even though we may not have been able to see a certain event coming, what can we learn from it to help us see what is coming next? Ironically, it is in debunking our idea that the *past* is knowable that the *future* becomes more knowable because we are open to a deeper learning we may have missed had we not been so sure about our ideas. Crazy, right?

PRACTICE Illuminating Biases

Gaining awareness of our patterned shortcuts and biases helps us illuminate the places where we go blind. Let's work with that now.

Recall a decision you are making or have just made, or an opinion you hold, and ask yourself:

1 *As I reflect upon this decision or opinion, am I accounting for what I don't know?*

2 *Is there a story I'm trying to create to make this decision or belief feel right and true?*

3 *If I move beyond my surface ideas and biases and through to what I most deeply know to be true, what do I realize?*

This third question is important because it speaks to the intuition and knowing that emerge when we see past and through our ideas and biases, and it surfaces what is currently hidden to us. We can use all these questions to open to a larger realm of possibility while perhaps finding a more balanced, spontaneous, and creative answer. However, we need to be at least a little comfy with ambiguity and uncertainty, and let go of trying to be an expert who has everything right. Easier said than done—I get it! Just think of an opinion that you don't want to let go of. It is *so* true and right, it makes you feel safe, and it makes your world feel organized. What if you loosened up on that one too? What would happen?

Increasing Bandwidth for Ambiguity

It's a lot to ask, uncovering the way these biases and filters form our blindness, and recognizing that things are more fluid than we thought. In a way, though, we can't afford not to. If we opt for the safety and security of our (possibly inaccurate) fixed ideas, we can cause suffering in our own and others' lives, whether it is apparent to us or not. This kind of security comes at a cost because somehow life has a way of not working well when we do this. It's like that algorithm idea—if we input faulty data, it starts skewing in the wrong direction.

Sensing ambiguity can be destabilizing if you're not used to it. For example, let's say that upon questioning your fixed ideas about your job you realize you are deeply unhappy at work. You've resisted acknowledging this because you like having a predictable income and your family relies on you. Your fixed idea that everything was great was working for you, and now you are seeing the reality of how you feel. There's something to be said for denial: suppressing this type of realization helps you survive. But telling yourself the truth and seeing through your fixed ideas does not mean you have to act on this new information—it just means you are no longer blind to it. That's what I mean by letting in a little ambiguity. You can stay in your job if your circumstances are such that you need to, but now that you're aware of your deeper dissatisfaction, you can meet yourself kindly and see what actions you can take to help you feel more satisfied there. Up until now, thinking everything was peachy seemed to work, but you realize that you felt dead inside, and now that you are in touch with your dissatisfaction you feel more alive, and more yourself. You are at the edge of your own horizon, peering into the unknown, and it can be a deeply alive place to be. We live in paradoxes, and that's part of the beautiful mess of being human.

Questioning biases and opening to a larger, more nuanced story don't have to destabilize us. Coming out of denial doesn't mean we need to act on our feelings. Rather, it can help us make wiser, more informed decisions and be more compassionate and understanding. It takes practice and experience to trust yourself enough to open to what you don't know, and realize that it's safe and important to do so. But don't worry—you're not going to die if you admit you don't have a clue! You don't have to exert effort all the time to check whether you are believing something untrue. Hacking these biases sets you up for a different autopilot: it opens you to the unknown and in doing so you move the arrow from blindness to mindful flow. It doesn't take much more than that!

The Flow State

Flow, which we've touched on before, is a state of effortless mastery in navigating the vicissitudes of life, and it comes through deep concentration and connection to our inner life. You know those moments when you're singing or dancing or building a table or sewing or making love and you lose yourself? When you sustain focused attention but there's no exertion of self-control—and hence no sense of a separate "me" doing a task? In that flow state, you are not trying to figure out how to be; you simply are. It is second nature because it's the most natural thing. You don't have to be doing something "right" or be an expert at it, yet you are fully engaged in the process without the typical filters that block your natural way of being. That's the mastery. The part of your mind that creates stories and hallucinations drops away, along with the *will* to be focused (you are just naturally focused without trying) and you are *in the flow*. It's the place where skills meet challenges and you can have effortless control without trying to remind yourself to be controlled.

You may have watched an athlete or a chef in this state, or felt it yourself. Talk about easy on the brain! If you stop and try to think about what you're doing while in flow, you're likely to lose it or become self-conscious and make errors. Think of golfers who are asked to describe their swing—when they try to use their slow-thinking system to reflect upon what they're doing, they mess up![11] To not have to deliberately control our attention yet have utter concentration on, and hence "control" of, a task is the essence of what we love and envy as humans; the flow state is the holy grail for anyone, from athletes and tech engineers to dancers. It releases us from having to use up valuable energetic resources to exert self-control (telling ourselves to pay attention and focus), and we have an effortless level of surrender and therefore mastery, so we veritably float through our experience. It's extremely pleasurable. We aren't unnecessarily using up glucose stored for other important brain tasks and we have extra energy and attention freed up to be here now!

Now, what does all this have to do with blind spots?

High Performance in the Ordinary

Blind spots (especially our core blind spot, which we will get to later in the book) keep us from experiencing the flow state in our everyday lives. This is because they cause us to make assumptions that block our spontaneity and engagement with life—without even realizing it.

Anyone can access the flow state, but it is typically associated with high-performance athletes like Kevin Pearce. Pearce was a champion snowboarder with a bright future in the Olympics when, while doing a 360-degree spin on a hill in Utah, he suffered a horrible accident. He slammed his head into a half-pipe, was airlifted to a hospital, and went into a coma. He suffered a traumatic brain injury (TBI) and was wheelchair-bound for several months. Since then he has rehabilitated and gotten back on his snowboard, but life will never be the same for him. So he has dedicated his life to cultivating TBI awareness through mindfulness and yoga with an organization he created called LoveYourBrain.

I had the opportunity to have a conversation with the cheerful, funny, and blunt (thanks to his accident) Kevin and his easygoing brother Adam. They are quite a pair, and are both interested in looking at the links between meditation and the flow state. Kevin's persistent and impassioned inquiry around the topic led him to ask these questions: "How do I get back to the flow state I had while snowboarding? I was in flow for weeks at a time!" and "How can you have flow when you're not in such an extreme state of agility in your sport—how can it be there in the simpler things in your life?" He had linked the activity of pro snowboarding with the flow state because his level of skill in it was off the hook, as were his utter ease and grace when he was in his pre-accident prime. Now he was challenged by his idea that flow can only be achieved at similarly high levels of physical skill, although he had experienced it in yoga. Flow is almost synonymous with terms like *peak performance* and *peak experience*, and is rarely applied to something like walking down the street or doing the dishes.

Flow can come after years of practice—think Yo-Yo Ma playing cello, where the music seems to be simply and effortlessly moving through him—and it can also come in a moment of insight, unexpectedly. One of my biggest life insights surfaced when I was simply staring at a wall, in what you could say was an experience of total flow. All sense of separation between myself and the wall dissolved, and I had a strong sense of the effortlessness of being, without any of the usual filters. In the same way that someone might say, "I lost myself in the music," I could say, "I lost myself staring at a wall."

I mention this because we hold the flow state out to be something "way out there" that is hard to get to, beyond reach, and only for hardcore athletes or musicians, someone like Yo-Yo Ma with tens of thousands of hours of experience. My supposition, though, is that skill and challenge can match each other in *any* situation, however mundane, if you have the quality of being fully aware and awake in the moment. If you walk down the street aware of your feet moving, your inner body sensations, a sense of the world around you, and your thoughts and emotions coming and going, the smells and sounds and colors vividly present, you are likely to experience something like flow, especially if you aren't exerting effort to achieve it. You become like a wide-eyed traveler in and through your experience, aware of how much there is that you do not know, yet closer somehow to your raw firsthand understanding of your own precious life and that of those around you.

To me, the "coherent stories" that come from a state of flow seem closer to the "real" story, like seeing and feeling it from the inside with a 360-degree view. They feel less filtered, and less blind, like the octopus without a blind spot. How much better is that than walking down the street clutching your phone close to your chest, in total contraction, worried about something that has never happened and completely out of touch with your body and your surroundings?

Remember how our fast-thinking system runs automatically? So much of what we do and think we understand happens on autopilot, and in this way we sleepwalk through our lives. It's in applying aware-ness and awakeness to our ordinary, everyday moments that we can *consciously experience* life, surfacing what is hidden and bringing it into the light, experiencing a quality of flow and ease amid any life cir-cumstance. Those moments of being lost in contracted worry or false stories become like signs pointing toward home, inviting our attention into a deeper alignment with what is real and true in our lives.

It's important to note that identifying those biases that blind us is especially crucial when the stakes are high—when we're in real danger but may not know the source. (Remember the tiger in the forest?) In the twenty-first century, the risks are often highest when we drive ourselves into the stress response by holding on to coherent stories that are untrue; they form the building blocks of suffering. Opening to the unknown doesn't turn us into doormats, but it does upend our idea that we are always right, and it opens the way for the alleviation of stress and suffering. Admitting we are fallible and increasing our tolerance of and bandwidth for ambiguity when the personal and emotional stakes are high will help us not only make more exact and wise decisions, but also tap into the state of flow. When unconscious biases and blocks are illuminated, we are no longer hindered by them. In this sense, the surfing of the unknown brings about a release of self-control and an increase in self-trust and connection with life around us, and openness to discovering our blind spots. It's not about perfection or being an expert; it's about feeling all of life moving through you—like Kevin effortlessly being snowboarded as he winds his way down a mountain, or Copernicus following the thread of inquiry to a concept that changed the world.

Now let's get some practice in letting go and being in flow.

PRACTICE   Allowing

- Reflect upon what is presently causing you the most stress in your life. Maybe it's a situation at work or a worry about a loved one, or an entrenched conflict or addiction that you can't seem to get out of. Take a moment to—remember welcoming?—welcome this place that is scary or challenging and causes you stress.

- Allow it to be here as it is for a moment and notice the landscape: how you feel, what you think, and any tension in your body.

- Now see if you can loosen your grip on your ideas about this situation: thoughts about how you or others should be different, or your opinions about who or what is to blame. What happens? When you can relax and open even a little bit as you are experiencing this stressful area of your life, you are waking up.

- Bring a quality of kindness to your experience, just as it is, and see if you can, just for a moment, open to a larger view—that there is more to this that you don't see—so you can relax your viewpoint.

- To build a sense of self-trust, repeat to yourself: "I can meet each moment as it comes with a wise response and I don't need to grip so tightly. I can relax and trust."

- Notice what you experience.

PRACTICE Opening to Flow

After you have done the allowing practice, here's an exercise to help you open up to flow.

- Sit in a comfortable position. Take a moment to feel a 360-degree awareness of your inner and outer environment. Sense your feet or legs on the ground, where you are in space—the room, the park, the beach. Let it all in at once: the outer landscape and its shapes, colors, outlines.

- Now pay attention to just your inner landscape: body sensations, emotions, and the thoughts and ideas swirling around in your mind.

- Zoom in more closely on one body sensation—such as the feeling in the palms of your hands or your heartbeat—and then zoom out, sensing the whole body at once. Allow everything to be there without need to change, fix, or figure anything out.

- Continue doing this, zooming in and out on one particular body sensation, going back and forth between it and the felt sense of your whole body at once.

- Now zoom in on your immediate environment. Find a color, sound, or shape. For example, the birdsong outside your window or the color of the carpet.

- Zoom out now with your attention, all the way into the room or outdoor environment. Zoom back in on the color, sound, or shape, and then again zoom out, including everything in the space and your body sitting there, all the way up into the atmosphere—through the ceiling or clouds and far into the sky and beyond—taking in everything at once, while still feeling yourself sitting and experiencing it all.

- Allow a sense of yourself as fully present, and a quality of stillness in your body, awake to the vastness of your surroundings from the point where you are sitting all the way out into space. Let go of any habit to control yourself or create a sense of separation between you and your environment, and be yourself, right where you are. This is flow.

- Catch that sense of flow, and follow it. Let it take you. Let go. Notice what happens.

- Now reorient, feeling your feet on the ground and your body alive and well as you become aware of your immediate surroundings.

- Bring this feeling into the rest of your day, carrying this sense of well-being and ease, and lack of self-consciousness. See what happens when you tune in to the greater environment around you, from moment to moment.

4

CHOOSE YOUR OWN ADVENTURE
Discovering Personalized Core Beliefs

WHEN I WAS GROWING UP, Choose Your Own Adventure books were all the rage. It was one of the most popular children's series in the 1980s and 1990s, featuring a new style of novel: the reader entered the narrative as the main protagonist and could "choose her own adventure" by deciding which story to follow from a list of options. So "If you want to go visit the museum with Fred, turn to page 70. If you want to leave Fred behind and travel to Paris alone, turn to page 145." The books created a palpable sense of the unpredictability and spontaneity of stories and their various routes and endings, depending on the reader's choice.

I loved this. And now I see that it's a helpful metaphor for our lives: we have choices all along the way that could bring us to radically different journeys and endings. If we could only approach our own stories with the same amount of curiosity and fun with which we read a book!

We've discussed how we blink out attentionally and can be blindly driven in our thinking by unconscious mental shortcuts and the stories we tell ourselves as a result. But what about our biggest story, the one closest to our core? In what ways are we blind to the most central story in the "choose your own adventure" of our lives, and how is that story driving us and impacting our choices and behaviors? What lies at the heart of our most stubborn blind spots? If we discover it, can we find a more curious, open, and adventurous way to navigate the choices we face?

Russian Dolls

I have noticed something about myself and the people around me—and it applies across cultures. Despite our varying degrees of aptitude, success, mental health, and socioeconomic status, our blind spots are typically tied to an imbalanced and mistaken set of unconscious beliefs about "me" and the world around "me". These beliefs are often stacked like Russian dolls, one within the other. They can be biologically driven, culturally driven, collectively driven, environmentally driven, family driven, and individually driven. They may be formed during a small and insignificant moment, yet they create large gaps in awareness that we carry with us through life. A core belief about yourself as simple as "I'm a fraud" can wreck your life because of the ways in which it drives you to filter your experience. When you see all the way into and through your core blind spot—this idea of "me" at the center of "my" world and its associated beliefs and patterns that define "me"—you can unhook from these drives that cause so much unnecessary suffering.

Collective Stories

Although they have unique expression in each of us according to our personal experience, our core beliefs and patterns come from the collective. In that sense, they aren't personal. *There is nothing new under the sun.* A Taiwanese business person, Nigerian city mayor, and a high schooler in the United States of America can all hold the same belief about being a fraud and worry that if they are found out—if people really see who they are—they will be rejected. Certain cultures apply specific signatures to the beliefs they pass down generation to generation, yet we all face thoughts and ideas that come from the collective as we are raised and emerge into adulthood, no matter the culture. Core beliefs are handed down to us. They are influenced by our gene expression, the way we are parented, and our culture, and they are processed through our unique biological, psychological, and chemical makeup. They are typically based on feelings of lack (*I don't have what I need*—safety, security, acceptance, love) or deficiency (*Something is wrong with me*—inadequacy, unworthiness, being flawed).

These beliefs aren't original, but they can feel true at the core of who we are, and they seem to define us personally. Even if we know better, we can still believe them, and they will drive us from beneath our conscious awareness.

Imagine going through your whole life blindly believing *I'm not good enough* or *I'm not safe* as a primary motivating driver while you navigate your experience. The adventures you choose will be colored by your assumptions and can have a massive impact on the journey of your life. This is why it is vital to peer beneath the hood and gain insight into the central stories that drive us. How do these stories form blind spots that become embedded into our psyche's operating system?

Where It Starts

When you are young and something distressing happens in your environment—perhaps you fall down and your caregiver doesn't attend to your pain, or you get bullied on the playground and nobody comes to your rescue emotionally or physically, or something far worse—your body and mind register that *something is off*. This could take the form of feeling a sense of hurt or discomfort, a contraction in your belly or chest, along with the emotion of anger or sadness. If no one is there to listen to or soothe you, or if you get punished for expressing these emotions, you may feel like you want to hide all of these feelings away. That's how a blind spot starts.

Emotions, physical sensations, beliefs, and thoughts are information, and our bodies are exquisitely built feedback mechanisms designed to take in that information and both alert us to danger and signal comfort and ease. This information guides us, letting us know when we can relax and when we must be alert to threats, and helps us feel and sense our experience. As adults, when something difficult happens, we get to choose our own adventure: we have the *option* to register the information our environmental and bodily cues give us (*Ouch! Something is wrong or off*) and choose to take an action to address it without personalizing it and turning it into a belief about our own self-worth. Not that most of us do that, but we do have the *capability* to. In the emotional intelligence world, it's called utilizing the skills of self-awareness and self-regulation to take wise and discerning action.

For instance, say Alice is in a meeting and someone there discredits her ideas about a project and then makes jokes about her inability to complete it. For Path 1 of choose your own adventure, turn to page 70! Alice feels the hurt and anger as she hears the words, and without pushing down that felt experience, she defends herself against the bully, asks for help from other team members, and does what she can to ensure she is protected from an attack like that happening again by bringing the matter to her boss's attention. She recognizes that her colleague is feeling insecure and trying to compete with her for the team's attention because he has a blind spot: a belief that *he's* unworthy. So he acts out with bravado to gain attention in order to be valued, and to not be blamed (at least that is what she can gather from what she sees).

Or Alice can make the ever-so-innocent and common mistake that something is wrong—with *her*! Path 2 of the adventure: turn to page 145! Her colleague discredits her ideas in the meeting and Alice feels helpless and shamed, pushing down her vulnerability with thoughts like *I'm no good, I can never do anything right. Everyone is out to get me.* It hurts too much to feel the pain of being discredited and the emotions that arise in the face of that, and rather than simply feeling what is there and finding an appropriate action, as she would by taking Path 1, she pushes her emotions down and has looping, judgmental thoughts about herself. She fosters the blind spot she has carried with her throughout her life, which, conveniently enough in this scenario, is that nobody ever listens to her and she'll never be heard no matter what she says. She starts to dread work, speaks less often in meetings, and hides her ideas in case they may set her up for attack. This version of the story tends to be a lot longer—and its plot is bumpy and confusing. The irony is that she isn't listening to *herself*. If she took a pause and stopped to do so, she would see her blind spot, hear the message coming from her shadowed psyche, and find creative, empowered solutions to her present-day work scenario.

However innocent it is to feel shame in a moment of helplessness, it can cause a lot of suffering when we *don't* see that we feel shameful, because in pushing that feeling down we are really letting it run the show. We think we've hidden our shame but instead it becomes an unrecognized driver of our behavior—it gets bigger and louder when we try to avoid it. But the shame is actually so nonthreatening at heart! It's simply a message from the body that something in the environment feels "off" or "wrong."

Yet fueled by the hurt that the workplace bully inspired, and because it feels so darn personal, *Something is wrong* becomes *Something is wrong with* me. *I'm not okay as I am.* And now we are headed off on our *mis*-adventure! We push down our vulnerable feelings and try to make our way through the situation as best we can, but we are out of touch with our own power and agency when we do so. If we've been doing this for our whole lives, it's hard to gain visibility into that core blind spot—it's the filter for our experience. It was the sense we could make from our environment when we were young, but it doesn't make sense anymore and it blinds us. *Bless our hearts.*

After, say, a conversation has gone sideways, the original piece of information—not good or bad, just data from the environment—may elicit a contraction in the belly. After watching the evening news, it may show up as a constriction of fear in the chest. But whatever the sensation may be, if we listen and pay attention to these physical cues, we can then find an action that will return us to equilibrium or harmony. This is why mindfulness practices that slow us down and build self-awareness, helping us get in touch with our body's cues, are so supportive in the discovery of our blind spots.

When Alice responded to her internal cues by taking Path 1, that meant she didn't need to bring work home with her. She wasn't immune to the hurt she experienced, but she was aware of her blind spot as well as her colleague's, and she didn't need to act hers out. Instead she used the information her body was giving her to abide in and speak from a place of power, not fear, and gained the respect of her peers and boss. This led her back into feelings of ease and confidence. Path 2, in contrast, created ongoing stress and suffering—internal and external—and kept those old ideas alive and well. They were so believable that she didn't even know she was blind, and the adventure she chose for herself was no fun at all.

Homeostasis—the Quest for Balance

Most organisms are constantly looking for a way to return to and support balance, something called *homeostasis*. We regulate variables—the changeable aspects of our experience—so we can keep a stable and consistent navigation as we flow through life. When we get knocked off center we develop various strategies to come back "home" to homeostasis, or a place of inner stability. Some of those strategies are wise and discerning, like using mindfulness tools to have self-compassion and gain insight into a situation, taking an appropriate action that brings us back home to balance. Some strategies, however, began when we were young and helped us cope but don't work that well anymore, like blaming ourselves in response to a challenging moment or distracting ourselves with addictive behavior. This keeps us out of balance and unstable in our navigation of life because our actions come from a blind spot and are out of alignment with who we really are at our essence. Our blind spots lurk in the "adventures" or strategies that we persist in using even though they don't work for us any longer. The good news is that we can spot them because they tend to hide in the moments where we find ourselves out of balance and thrown off our center, or where we distract ourselves from our own pain and hurt.

Let's return to the example of being hurt as a kid because we didn't receive adequate attention from our caregivers or community. Our environment gave us a signal that something was out of balance. In this case, our caretakers weren't meeting our fundamental needs for attunement, attention, or physical comfort. We were helpless at that time to think this through and take action. And even if we could have, most of us were way too young to know the best action to take, as Alice was able to do as an adult. She turned her *capability*—using her slow-thinking systems to question and slow down her automatic beliefs—into a *capacity*. Her response in not taking the affront personally (even though it was hurtful) was automatic and effortless because she had, perhaps through practice and insight, understood that the best action to take was meeting the moment with kindness and curiosity and finding an appropriate response without getting lost in her blind spot, which was now out of the shadows for her. In this way, yes, she felt it; yes, it hurt; but no, it didn't deepen her blind spot.

If you replay the movie of your life starting at the beginning, how did you learn to cope? Did you repress your feelings and needs? Did you stop listening to yourself because others weren't listening to you? Did you act tough on the outside and feel vulnerable on the inside? When you play back what you pushed down or ignored, can you see the early formation of a blind spot you are still working to see past today?

The truth is that often as children something in our environment *is* too much, something *is* not enough, and something *is* wrong. That part, we get right. Our detour on the choose your own adventure path is that we make it about *ourselves*! No wonder even as adults we can constantly misinterpret the information and feedback we receive from the world and our own bodies as we flow, bumble, and charge through life. We mistakenly personalize it, don't we? Something feels off or wrong, and we push down our feelings of vulnerability, shame, or hurt—feelings that are common to all of us—to appear a certain way and hold up our idealized self-view, personalize it to *Something is wrong with me*, and the rest is history. (Unless our version of blindness points to the world around us: *Something is wrong with you*. Even there, it originates in us and we project it outward, so the same basic dynamic is occurring.) Our idealized self-image becomes a weight we carry around with us, and we try to unload it or hide from it, or act cool when we don't feel cool at all. Picture all of us humans—billions of us together—each carrying around on our shoulders our personal idealized self-images and beliefs as baggage that doesn't even belong to us to begin with!

It's important to note that we don't personalize only what is hard or negative in our environment; sometimes we personalize the good. *Something is right* information can work this way. We had a successful presentation or a moment of deep connection with a loved one. Our environment, often via others' praise or gratitude, gives us positive feedback, and what do we do with it? *I'm awesome!* It's great to have a positive self-image and celebrate accomplishments. So far, so good.

However, let's say we grew up with an internalized voice that got handed down to us from our parents, or another important caretaking figure, that tells us we're *not* worthy and that if people really knew us they would find out we are a fraud. That anything other than perfect isn't good enough. And as a result we now carry around a fragile, insecure, or inflated self-image that is dependent for its happiness and survival on people saying we are awesome. If we're doing that, what about that next presentation in the boardroom? Or the next moment with our loved one when we don't show up perfectly—as what poet John O'Donohue called a "human potentialized hot tub Californian human being"?[1] Now we add a misperception—a belief—that we *should* be a certain way, and that is another manifestation of a blind spot in operation. We are convinced we need to live up to how awesome we once perceived ourselves to be, or how someone else thought we were.

Have you ever put that kind of pressure on yourself? All for the sake of protecting an image that isn't even real in its definition of who you are at your essence (even though, when you believe it, it surely does feel real). We all know the disappointment that occurs when we don't match up to our idealized view of ourselves, and the continuous self-improvement project that can result. Like pushing yourself to get two advanced degrees just so your father will (finally) be proud of you—something he's been holding out in front of you like a carrot all your life—while disowning the fact that deep down you hate academia. Or you see yourself as a loving, kind person, but when you treat someone rudely, you blame them and block out or justify your actions because your behavior doesn't fit your self-image. These are ways we blink out on the truth and the impacts of our actions.

Can you see how this (albeit innocent and learned) behavior of personalizing information from our inner and outer environment can be so costly? My own beliefs that drove me to avoid vulnerability and pain caused a lot of suffering and anxiety, and formed neat little blind spots that I was oblivious to . . . until I wasn't. Seeing the core beliefs we carry and how innocently we formed them—they were never really ours to begin with—is a courageous step toward illuminating the shadows and becoming more whole. We then can own who we are and what has happened to us, and create empowering stories in our lives.

Perfectly Flawed

The great news is that we really can choose our own adventure, and navigate in a lighthearted, open way. It doesn't have to be hard; we just need the willingness and capacity to look directly at our blind spots, illuminate them, learn and grow from the gifts we find, and let ourselves be ordinary human beings, off the hook from having to hold up and defend an image of ourselves that we've been carrying around forever.

Even people we admire and respect for their wisdom and character—think Mother Teresa, Desmond Tutu, the Dalai Lama, Jane Goodall—are "flawed" human beings. To be human is to be flawed, imperfect, a jumbled mix of contradictions, sometimes feeling superior, sometimes inferior. It's people like these, who are well practiced with the full spectrum of being human, that we are drawn to and want to emulate. These folks have graduated from being stuck in extremes, and from identifying with just one part of themselves. The Dalai Lama, through his devoted practice as a student of life, knows this whole spectrum of motivations within himself and brings a playful attitude of kindness and curiosity to what and whom he meets. *He isn't perfect; he just isn't fooling himself.* In a way, seeing blind spots is a great undoing: it unhooks us from everything we're not, and then we have a chance to discover who we really are. This isn't something to be achieved in the future; it is here right now, as you harness the power of being awake and alive to what is actually occurring in front of (and within) you.

Most of the wise, compassionate, and "awake to life" people I have met are direct, lighthearted, and *very* human. They know that they don't know, and there is a deep and settled realization in that. It's as if their idealized self has dropped away. They are no longer defending a "me" that was built on false beliefs and then obscured by blind spots. They aren't driven by anyone else's or their own *ideas* anymore but instead by reality, and each moment becomes spontaneous and honest, and in flow. They still have blind spots that come into view or that they now see and are working with, but it's all part of the unfolding story and it doesn't need a central character to defend.

Having the courage to ask these questions about our core beliefs and how we hold the world together with our sense of self can invite us to lay down the weapons we carry to defend an image of "me" that isn't as real and solid as we think it is. Sometimes, though, we need a little support to come out of our protective hiding places and see things clearly.

The Defense of the Loyal Soldier

Hiroo Onoda was an Imperial Japanese intelligence officer who was stranded on the Philippine island of Lubang when World War II ended. He never got the memo that the war was over (and never believed leaflets that were dropped from the sky announcing the war's end, thinking they were enemy propaganda). Together with a small group of soldiers, he continued to obey his orders to defend Japan for years. Fast-forward *twenty-nine years* and he was the only one left of the small group, still living on that island and still defending Japan from its enemies. In 1974, Norio Suzuki, a young Japanese explorer and adventurer, set out to find Hiroo after reading about him in history books. Astonishingly, he managed to discover him, and avoided being killed by him, by telling him that the emperor was worried about him and wanted to talk. They became friends, and Norio learned just what Hiroo needed in order to stop believing this delusion. *He needed to be relieved of his duty.*

Norio returned to Japan, found Hiroo's former commander, who was by then an old bookseller, and brought him along with a delegation back to the Philippines. Hiroo was informed that Japan had ceased combat and that he needed to place himself under this officer's command. That was all he needed to hear—he laid his weapons down willingly. To help Hiroo transition back to civilian life, the Japanese people gave him a hero's welcome, celebrating his allegiance to their country, despite the fact that it was no longer considered an honorable war. It marked a shift for the "loyal soldier"—he could stop protecting and defending now, *and* he was welcomed home.

We are all like Hiroo in some way, blindly defending something that does not need defending anymore and that isn't what we think it is: this thing we call "me" made up of outdated beliefs and images that aren't true but that we haven't had reason to question. When we lay our weapons down—the strategies we use to defend—and stop believing the false core stories we hold about ourselves, we open to the discovery of our most precious gifts and find who we are at an essential level. We are way more open and spacious than we think! When we discover this, all of the ups and downs—the vicissitudes of life—flow in and through us and we learn to more fully participate in the story of our lives. We bring curiosity and humor to the choices we make in the choose your own adventure we are living, and find a sense of flow and ease in the journey, no matter what is unfolding.

Welcome Yourself Home

You can do the same thing the Japanese people did for Hiroo: throw a party for your loyal soldier. Welcome it home and into the light. Let it know it needs to put its weapons down because it's defending something that does not need protection anymore, something based on a core story that may not hold up under inspection! The loyal soldier can still be part of you but can serve in a new way, reminding you when you're believing something that really isn't true. It can come home, but seriously, its job ended *so twenty-nine years ago.*

The key player in the Japanese story of the loyal soldier, to me, was Norio Suzuki. He bravely risked his life to hack his way through an unknown jungle just to rescue one lonely, loyal soldier who had been lost for years! He must have been more curious than fearful, and this says a lot about how we too can be inquisitive as we shine a light on these hidden, potentially scary areas. A side note: Norio died years later in the Himalayas searching for the Abominable Snowman! I can't help but think he died happily, driven by curiosity and love of the search.

•

The following practice is intended to help you get unstuck from a core story that you were blind to and lost in, and that may be an integral part of your blind spot. It is not intended to push out the so-called "negative." In seeing clearly you don't need to push anything out, because everything occupies its rightful place, coming and going in a larger spectrum of awareness. These beliefs, and their attendant emotions, are messengers asking for some love and care! If this feels cheesy and navel-gazey, no problem—in a way, it is—but I've found that applying insight and practice to our blind spots can be immensely powerful in unlocking our unconscious cognitive patterns. So hang with it if you can. You are illuminating your blind spots! Next time you get stuck in a story, let yourself question it in this way and see what happens. When you see through your personalized core beliefs, you come to realize that this thing called "me" at the center of your world is more dynamic and fluid than you imagined, which opens access to a whole new way of being: spontaneous, lighthearted, and in touch with the beautiful mess that is the unfolding story of your life.

PRACTICE **Find Your Blind Spot Story**

- Take a moment to think of a core negative belief you hold to be true about yourself. If you can't find one, think of one you have about someone else—and write it down: I'm _____ or I'm not _____. I'll give a few examples: *I'm not free to be who I am. I'm not worthy. I'm a piece of doo-doo. I'm amazing and everyone else sucks. I don't fit in.* Choose a belief that hits home and feels believable. Mine is something like *I'm not safe.* You don't have to believe it all the time (I certainly don't) but find one that, when you do believe it, is super believable! Everyone has a core story like this, so give yourself time to see what it is for you.

- Then notice how you feel in your body when you believe this to be true. If you're a breathing human being, when you take the story to be true, you'll find a contraction somewhere in your body.

- Continue the exercise. Maybe there's a contraction in your belly or chest or shoulders when you take this thought to be true. You might feel a few emotions associated with the belief of this thought, such as shame, unworthiness, sadness, or anxiety.

- Take a moment to notice what happens when you believe the thought without judgment, without making yourself wrong, without trying to fix it or make it go away. How do you act when you believe this story about yourself, such as *Nobody will ever understand me* or *I'm not free to be me* or *I'm not safe*?

- What do you experience in your body? Notice any contraction or tension, and simply allow it to be here without refusing it or being overwhelmed by it. If at any point this does become overwhelming, return to the Five Mindful Breaths practice and skip this exercise, or come back to it later when you feel drawn to it.

- Now ask yourself: *If this belief weren't here, what would be here?* In other words, *What would I be believing instead? What is a truer story?* Is it something like "I'm free" or "I'm understood" or "I'm loved"? How do you feel in your body when you believe that thought? Is there a palpable relief and relaxation?

- Or perhaps that new story is just not believable. No problem. Hold both beliefs in your awareness: the "negative" one and the "positive" one. You aren't trying to replace one with the other; you are seeing that they live on a spectrum and that one can't exist without the other. As you feel and recognize both beliefs at the same time, what do you notice? What do you see that you didn't see before? Allow yourself to be surprised.

- As you relax and hold both stories at once (and take your time here), is there any message or insight that emerges? There's no need to force this; just let it come naturally. The truth and deep insights emerge naturally when they aren't forced. You are surfacing the filters through which you see so you can bring what is in shadow into the light.

- Perhaps you are holding two beliefs like *I'm not okay as I am* and *I'm perfect just the way I am*. Perhaps the deeper truth that emerges is *I am free to be me*. You never know what you will discover, so let yourself be open to what you find.

- Then go for a long walk without your smartphone. Notice what arises in your mind and heart, the color of the leaves on the trees, the smell of the flowers, and the feel of the ground under your feet.

- In opening to what you don't now see, you are much farther along than before. Perhaps your belief was *I have to be perfect for others to love me* and the opposite was *I'm wonderful as I am*. When you stayed with it, perhaps a deeper insight arose such as *I give myself permission to be all of me in each moment* or *I trust myself to be me. I don't have to perform for others—I can let go.*

- If this exercise doesn't resonate, then ask these two questions: *What is my core negative belief about myself or the world?* And then follow it up with: *What is more true, that I know deep down?*

- One more hack: Does your blind spot come from lack (*I don't have what I need*—safety, security, acceptance, love) or deficiency (*Something is wrong with me*—inadequacy, unworthiness, being flawed)? This may help you pinpoint your personalized core belief if you can't quite make it out right now.

5

THE FULL SPECTRUM

Welcoming Emotional Blind Spots

The word "happy" would lose its meaning
if it were not balanced by sadness.

CARL JUNG[1]

ONCE WHEN I was teaching at a retreat, a woman expressed that over the years she had often thought about ending her life. She had come to the retreat out of desperation, seeking some answers. She had a daughter and husband at home who loved and supported her, but she was in a lot of pain. She had been distancing herself from her family because she felt so empty and miserable. After I invited the group to mindfully allow their experience to be just as it is, she raised her hand and said, "I feel anger come up when you invite us to welcome our experience. I feel like saying, 'Fuck that.'"

I gently asked, "Can you be with that anger for just a moment, if it feels okay?"

She took a pause to feel it, and then shared, "It just feels like a waste of time. It's like I don't value myself enough to even spend that kind of time with my experience."

She and I sat together with her anger and hurt, along with her ideas about her own self-worth, meeting it all on its own terms for a few minutes, just allowing it to be there—*welcoming* it. Then I led the group in a guided meditation in which I invited the participants to take part in a welcoming practice. Follow along as you read, and then try it for yourself.

PRACTICE   Welcoming Emotions

- Take a moment to welcome any emotions that may be knocking on your door.

- See what appears to you as you open the door to what is asking for your attention.

- Notice what emotion comes into the room and whether you can name it, such as *sadness* or *irritation*.

- How old is this emotion? What does it look like? How does it feel? What is it like to be with it without trying to make it go away or fix it?

- Linger in this slow, gentle inquiry and wait for what comes. Now feel free to ask it whether it needs anything right now that you could give, or if it has any other requests.

- Stay close to your experience, listening, and welcoming it to be here. No need to make it any different than it is. How does it feel to do this? Are there any actions you might take to give it what it needs or is asking for?

- Now let it know that you will return to it later if necessary, but you are going to say good-bye to it for now.

- Take a moment to reflect on this experience, and then bring your attention gently back to the present moment.

You can do this exercise with someone else too. Ask a friend you trust, "Hey, would you be willing to practice a few minutes of welcoming with me?" Then sit together and go through these same steps, and share whatever is weighing on your heart. Their job is just to listen and silently receive you, without interjecting or trying to fix or change you. They are there as a kind, welcoming presence for you.

Then switch, so they get a turn too. Just a couple of minutes of sharing in this way can be transformative because it bypasses our typical mode of communication and allows us to peer into the shadows where blind spots and their associated difficult emotions lurk.

At the retreat when we finished the practice, the woman began crying and offered that when she had invited her anger in, she saw that it was her seven-year-old self. She had gotten on the floor with her littler self and asked this anger what she needed. The little girl just wanted someone to play with! She didn't feel worthy of attention because she so often felt isolated and had long been angry about it, and that caused her to feel shut down. The woman imagined the two of them playing Legos together and had a fun, warm encounter. She reported through her tears that for the first time in ages she didn't have an empty, depressed feeling, and she couldn't wait to get back to her daughter so she could take her to the movies and play games with her, all from this new place of connection with herself.

Wow.

That is the power of welcoming emotional blind spots. It doesn't solve or take away problems, but it allows for closeness to what is present, and that power of presence and awareness can be transformative and healing. It gives us the opportunity to make commitments to our tender parts, and when we experience the power of this kind of meeting, we no longer want to leave ourselves behind. Our perceptive capacities go from fuzzy to high resolution in these moments of clarity and insight, bringing blind spots into greater focus and creating less resistance toward and avoidance of what we experience.

How do you welcome a difficult emotion? It's not as hard as you might think! The next time you feel overwhelmed, whether it's by stress, sorrow, disappointment, or even exuberance, stop and pause. Notice what happens when you look at it without trying to change it or see it as something it's not, and instead simply feel how you feel when you feel it. Notice the sensations in your body and anything else that is present, like other emotions as well, or related thoughts. The act of not refusing is an act of welcoming. You're not inviting it in so it can overtake you, although that might be your fear. The truth is, it's there anyway! (Of course, the caveat is that if you're experiencing something overwhelming, like trauma, it's wise to get help and support rather than try to barrel through it on your own. It's of primary importance that you are resourced enough internally to be able to meet and greet what arises. If you don't feel resourced, allow yourself to find support, and first build resilience by bolstering your inner sense of well-being and capacity to meet what comes.)

By welcoming a moment of difficulty or joy rather than refusing its presence, we blink *in* to our lives—attentionally speaking—and the result is powerful, allowing us to get in touch with what is actually there, see more clearly, and find the best response to the moment. In paying attention *with intention*, we move past preconception and distraction. This works with anything from physical pain to a fuzzy emotion or a deep existential question; it's all fair game in this process of welcoming what is present. Welcoming our emotional lives builds emotional intelligence and resiliency.

The Spectrum of Emotion

Every emotion exists on a spectrum; there are extremes at both ends and a long stretch of middle. This spectrum might range from despair to ecstasy, or heartbreaking disappointment to deep fulfillment. In this way, opposites exist together; they co-arise. Jealousy, for instance, holds the seed of its opposite: confidence and the willingness to stand in our own "one wild and precious life," as the poet Mary Oliver so aptly describes it.[2] We can't escape the spectrum of feelings, emotions, and ideas we experience. In a way, we hold everything inside us, whether or not we act it out or have access to it. We can't have cold without hot; it's only cold *in relation* to hot. In the same way, we can't have happiness without sadness; they are inextricably linked, and you could say they are flip sides of the same coin. If we can feel one end, we can feel all the way through to the other. Have you ever been so happy that you felt sad? Or so sad you felt happy? These emotions aren't fixed, solid entities. They range from one extreme to the other with many gradations in between.

The way to bring what is emotionally hidden into the light is to understand this spectrum and where our biggest blind spot falls on it, because that is the spot where we can get stuck and identified with one end of the spectrum—like, for example, a feeling of unworthiness. We can blindly organize our experience around one strong feeling and blink out on the range and nuance contained in our emotional lives. This makes us miss what's right in front of us: the precious message this emotion has been trying to communicate, such as its inverse: our incredible worthiness and value that we have pushed down. Isn't it ironic that the key to getting unstuck from an emotion lies in simply being with it and listening to its message? Yet we do everything we can to avoid what we feel because it seems "bad" or "wrong" or unwanted to us.

Resistance

Imagine that your neighbor knocked on your door and when you opened it you exclaimed, "Oh, it's *you!*" and slammed the door shut. This is what we do with the stuff we don't want to see—our anger, our shame, and even our happiness. The feelings these emotions evoke are too uncomfortable, or the emotions won't stop dropping by and we're annoyed that they're here so we push them out by ignoring them, or down by repressing them. There's a reason these emotions pop up: they carry a message. When we shut the door on them, we don't see them, but they're still standing on the front porch and will eventually knock again.

It's simple, but not easy, to learn how to feel emotions as sensation in our bodies and to work with emotions and thoughts skillfully, not trying to make them go away but getting close enough to our own life to find out what they're asking of us and guiding us toward. This doesn't mean we are jerked around by our emotions; quite the opposite. By welcoming and meeting them we can *stop* being jerked around.

Have you ever spent an entire Saturday frustrated and annoyed after a long week of work, nitpicking your partner and bossing your kids around? You may be ignoring the fact that you feel frustrated, but you're still acting out and other people feel the impact. One way to welcome your emotion in that moment is to notice that you're experiencing a difficult feeling, like anger or frustration, and observe how it feels in your body—maybe there's a contraction in your belly or chest. Allow it to be there without fighting against it, and notice how hard it is not to take it out on your family. Now let go of punishing the people around you for something that happened at another time and in another place, and find a kinder, more empathetic way to hold your own experience without needing to act it out. Own it, but don't get lost in it.

At other times it's important to sit with that feeling and work with it to glean the insights and messages it has for us. (*I'm still frustrated from my meeting on Tuesday with that board member and I haven't let it go. I may need to talk to a colleague. Or maybe I just have to accept the fact that this is a hard situation that will take a while to resolve so I can let it go and be present with my family. I'll shelve this for now because I just thought of a couple of actions I can take later to address the situation.*)

At yet other times, allowing that feeling to be there without either ignoring it or trying to do anything at all with it may be best. Remember the acceptance and love we yearn for? That's what moments filled with emotion are urging us to do: to simply be with our experience as it is, accepting and welcoming it with an awareness of the full spectrum of life in which the experience arises. When we do this, we have more access to the data in our field of awareness, our blind spots can come into the light, and we can find an action to take that will bring us back into balance and homeostasis: that will bring us home. Like a neighbor knocking on the door holding a letter, our feelings can contain important information. Our actions and responses are wiser and more thoughtful when we reach out to accept the message instead of slamming the door.

Often when we practice mindful welcoming or mindful awareness, we find that an aspect of our experience—an emotion like worry or insecurity—is simply asking for a little attention. Maybe part of us needs to be loved, held, hung out with, and not refused. We aren't typically taught to do those things; we have learned instead to run away from the hard stuff or numb it, change it, or try to fix it. It takes a lot of patience and presence to welcome what comes. To face a challenging situation and lean into our experience with kindness and curiosity, and meet ourselves moment to moment—just being with it. That is why mindfulness is a *practice* and a way of being and not a method to resolve, escape, or obscure the beautiful mess of our lives.

Can you see how welcoming can be a lens for looking at our blind spots, and in so doing, building emotional intelligence? When we welcome our experiences instead of judging, avoiding, or fearing them, we can see things more clearly, hear the messages our environment and experience have for us, and find a spontaneous, proper response to each moment. This is not a passive practice; it's an engaged and active way of taking part in our own story.

Freeing Energy and Attention

If we welcome unwanted or neglected feelings and free the energy that was bound up in those emotional blind spots—such as misperceptions, defending an idealized version of ourselves, or being preoccupied with the stress of life and lost in our emotions—and see things for what they are without resisting, managing, or controlling the experience, we find it easier to see important information. This is because we are connected to what is happening in the moment and less likely to misperceive our circumstances. This translates to a lot more well-being and flow.

Of course, this is *far* easier said than done. It's hard to see ourselves, especially our unconscious selves. For instance, let's say we hear from our husband, children, and coworkers in different ways that they see us as controlling; it's not easy to finally slow down and admit that, yes, we really have been controlling. But in welcoming our emotions around this, we might begin to see that *we* actually feel out of control and have been trying to manage everyone around us in order to calm ourselves down. Now we are in contact with what is real, and even though it doesn't feel good, it feels right and in a way, it's a relief. We can find the gift in it now because we are hot on the trail of what has been hidden.

That's an example of the benefit of being undefended and willing to listen; we can change from the inside, not because others need us to but because they see our emotional blindness and have the presence to point it out, and we have the presence to see and be with it in a curious way. It's how we cultivate self-awareness.

Opposites and Self-Awareness

Emotional intelligence is the capacity to know and understand our thoughts, feelings, and motivations. The key pillar of emotional intelligence is self-awareness, and we can't build self-awareness without *being in touch with the whole spectrum of emotions* and knowing and understanding the various ebbs and flows of our experience. It's easy to get lost or fused at one spot: for example, experiencing depression without any sense of contact with the other end of the spectrum, joy; or feeling anxiety without feelings of safety or ease. A spectrum implies two ends separated by a middle. And there's good news in that: if we're stuck at one end of the scale, we can find our way to the other end.

PRACTICE   Seeing the Spectrum

Here's how you can practice working with the spectrum of emotion to get unstuck from an extreme end.

- Think back to the most recent time you felt lost in an emotion and explore it. What was the emotion? What was your reaction? Did you distract yourself, or go into a pity party, or blame everyone else? Did it feel overwhelming or completely take over your experience? If so, that's a good sign you were stuck at one extreme, and looking across the whole spectrum to the other end can help you get unstuck.

- Welcome that emotion to be here as it is.

- Now take a moment to notice what the opposite of that emotion is. If it is sadness, for example, perhaps recall a sense of joy.

- Now feel both ends of this emotional spectrum at the same time. When you sense the full spectrum of your emotional experience, what do you notice?

It's important to understand what the opposite of an intense emotion is because it helps us to see the continuum it lives on and, in a way, its resolution. It helps us when we welcome the stuck emotion to be here because once we hang out with it long enough to see, we know it's not the only story. We can see better because we aren't lost in it, and paradoxically, when we can see its opposite, we are closer to the truth of it.

To offer another example, when I get lost in a moment of worry, I may be missing out on the contentment and safety that I *also* feel because my brain is being driven by the negativity bias. Welcoming the worry can help me bring the other end of the spectrum into my experience. You can do this even with what appear to be overwhelming emotions. Sometimes the volume is turned up on a certain emotion because there is a well-worn neural pathway of negativity and depression or anxiety, so it's easy to stay stuck in a loop of overwhelm. However, doing this simple practice can work wonders, because it gets you out of the story in your head and brings you right into the present moment, where you kindly greet yourself—even the part of yourself that is hoarse from all its noisemaking. Your nervous system calms down when you stop pushing yourself away.

Full Catastrophe Living

Jon Kabat-Zinn, who popularized the modern mindfulness movement, calls this welcoming of the entire spectrum "full catastrophe living." It's a full-hearted approach to life in which we mindfully stay with whatever life throws at us without getting lost. When you add presence and awareness to the mix, you automatically get unstuck, because you can see something from the outside even while you're meeting it on the inside. When we inquire into our experience and welcome it, we can move within the spectrum of emotions and train ourselves to get unstuck and see blind spots; we aren't fused at one end of the spectrum without a larger perspective. When we can see the whole, we catch more. Here's an analogy: If you're sitting in a crowded café scrolling through social media, look up from your phone and open your awareness, taking in the entire environment. When you are lost in a Twitter feed, you miss a lot.

The cost of what we miss is why it's so important to train our attention to be aware of what is present in any given moment. As soon as something like anger arises, we can get lost in it and act out *or* we can let it be there and fully feel it, and then feel its opposite and see what else may be there too—such as fear, confusion, or helplessness.

Your body holds the key here. The way to fully feel an emotion is to notice where and how you sense it in your body. When you're angry, maybe your shoulders and belly tense up and your body contracts. Notice those sensations without judging. If there is a story associated with the anger, don't get lost in it but let that be there as well. It's very simple, although not easy, to focus on sensations like tight shoulders, tense belly, or warm hands. You may think that meeting your emotions as a felt sense in your body needs to be more difficult than that, because you have an agenda of getting rid of the emotion and fixing yourself, or you think that if you "mindfully notice" the heck out of it, the emotion will go away. But simply feeling body sensations as you welcome emotions is the primary way to bring a sense of curiosity and kindness to your experience. The truth is that the only way we know we are angry or anxious or happy or sad is through bodily sensation! That is the information superhighway we wake up to as we learn to meet and greet our experience from moment to moment.

The way to feel an emotion's opposite on the full spectrum is to imagine how you might feel if it weren't there: maybe if you weren't anxious or sad, you'd feel ease or happiness. And how do those emotions show themselves in your body? Spacious, light, with a quality of relaxation in your belly and shoulders? The way to open to the full spectrum is to notice whether any other sensations in your body are calling to you as felt emotions lying beneath the surface. As you open, your body will naturally show you what is there. Then it's just wash, rinse, repeat.

Doing this in response to an emotion you have noticed may lead to an insight and an action you could take in response. Like saying to your partner when he walks in the room, "You know, I feel angry right now. I'm just acknowledging that. I think I may be hurt underneath." What a novel idea! There is also a simple power in noticing what's there while not getting involved in it—you can see the larger spectrum and you don't miss as much. Being aware of what is going on in your body and mind gives you more control of your life because you aren't being driven by what is in the shadows. You may think, *But if I get awake to all the stuff swirling around inside of me then I'll have to quit my full-time job and just sit there navel-gazing all day.* Well, you can check out whether that is true or not! You can see for yourself that welcoming emotions is not equal to becoming a basket case. My hunch, and experience, is that we don't have to do it all at once, and we have incredible capacity for gaining emotional intelligence, each at our own speed and skillfulness, with the result being a greater amount of freedom and happiness in our lives.

Find the Recycled Emotion in Your Body

"Recycled" emotions are the ones that keep coming back throughout your life, and they sometimes hold a key to discovering your blind spots. Is there an emotion that you have consistently felt over the course of your life? Mine is anxiety. Yours could be disappointment, or anger, a feeling of resistance to life, sadness, or confusion. What's important about recognizing these habitual emotional states for yourself is that they are usually paired with a belief about yourself, others, or the world around you, such as your core negative belief. And this recycled emotion may be hiding a blind spot that causes you to behave unconsciously in some way to meet those fundamental needs for acceptance, love, and connection (not to mention safety). In bringing emotions to light and welcoming them, you can make them into tools for finding what's holding you back. So let's get some practice using that tool.

PRACTICE   **Recycled Emotions**

- Reflect upon an emotion that is a trigger response for you in lots of different kinds of situations—your recycled emotion.

- Name the emotion: _____ *has resurfaced repeatedly through my life.*

- Name how it feels in your body and where it appears: *I feel this emotion in my* _____ *and the body sensation that goes along with it is* _____.

- Name the reaction: _____ *(tuning out, distracting, blaming others, blaming myself, getting lost, dissociating) is my typical response to feeling this emotion.*

- Allow yourself time to reflect upon what you discovered. *What is my deepest truth when I feel into the core of this emotion? What is it trying to tell me?* Let yourself listen for the message, and see what you discover.

- If you still feel stuck and that you haven't gained insight, then feel free to explore the emotion's opposite. If this emotion weren't here, what would be here instead? How would you be feeling in your body if this emotion kept coming back instead of the recycled one? Let yourself notice what you find when you do this practice with opposites.

What if that recycled emotion you've been feeling your whole life is a message waiting to be interpreted? A feeling of grief that you never felt as if you belonged, or a feeling of disappointment that people you have needed to count on let you down. What if this whole time it's been there, sometimes in the background, sometimes knocking at your door, asking for attention? There are always present-day circumstances that it gets affixed to, but it originated earlier in your life, so the encouragement is to go back there and listen to what it has been asking of you. So often that request in the form of a sad or hopeless feeling is simply to be heard, to be hung out with, and to just feel a sense of belonging with the rest of you. It's not usually complicated!

Our emotional blind spots form because we can't see the other end, or anywhere else, on the spectrum. For me, learning to feel anxiety as sensations in my body changed my life. That particular emotion drove me for years before I stopped to feel the sensations related to it. But the moment I did that, my world began to change. When I could experience anxiety as sensations—rapid heartbeat, sweaty palms, tense belly—I gained the distance I needed to see that they were coming and going in my experience. In naming them and getting to know them, I learned to catch panic in its early stages, before it reached the crescendo of terror, and I felt more intimate with and awake to my experience.

I also saw the stories I was creating in my mind as a by-product of feeling those sensations of anxiety, and traced the feeling back to its origins: how I had pushed it away because it hadn't been okay to feel it in those younger moments. When I woke up to that, I was no longer hostage to my emotional life because I saw it as an ally guiding me home to myself—a more integrated "me" that needed safety and security, and a holding presence of love during my challenging times. Until I paid somatic attention to my experience, all the cognitive therapy in the world couldn't have helped me. The trauma and anxiety were stuck in my body, and it was through my body that they were healed and welcomed home. One moment of welcoming the emotion and seeing what it wants and needs changes everything if you let it. It also reveals its opposite, offering a kind of a resolution because the full spectrum is now seen and integrated. This is what it looks like to bring emotional blind spots to the surface as we see and strip away filters. It's hard to sustain attention on two things simultaneously, such as two opposite feelings or thoughts—so it quiets the mind to see the full spectrum at once, allowing our body's innate wisdom to shine through.

Free Fall

There's a cartoon I like. The first panel shows a guy falling through space, screaming and wildly flailing his arms. The second panel is entitled "Two Weeks Later" and the guy is still falling through space but this time he's kicked back, his arms are crossed over his chest, and he's completely relaxed. When such radical free falling is paired with growing trust, it's life changing. And exploring emotional blind spots may lead us to interesting places we never thought we'd reach!

Let's face it: the unknown is scary. We do what we can to buffer against it—holding tightly to stories or trying to make everything fit into our beliefs—and rightly so. Our mental shortcuts help guide us in keeping it simple, and ignorance can be bliss, lending a form of balance. But who knew that a key ingredient in uncovering blind spots is to *increase* our bandwidth and capacity for the unknown? If we don't have that capacity, we aren't likely to be interested in seeing what's there, because it's uncharted territory and needs our presence at the edge of our moment-to-moment experience.

We can hang out and get stuck in one of these hidden places, sometimes for years, *blindly* driven by a belief or overwhelming emotion. We can also welcome what is there instead of refusing it and gain insight into the terrain, flowing with the difficulties of life. Can you see the difference? One way isn't better than the other or the right way to do it, but one surely causes less suffering.

The choice is ours. If we can see our emotions and our thoughts as coming and going within a larger space, we are less likely to get stuck and lose ourselves in a blind spot, and more likely to bring the blind spot into the light and learn something important.

●

In the next chapter we will move from exploring our attentional, emotional, and thinking blind spot patterns and dive into the interpersonal: blindness in love.

6

LOVE IS BLIND

First Impressions and Falling in Love

Love looks not with the eyes, but with the mind
And therefore is winged Cupid painted blind.
WILLIAM SHAKESPEARE, *A Midsummer Night's Dream*

THERE'S A GUY named Irving who regularly comes to my neighborhood café. His wife is Elizabeth. He's ninety-three, and she's about twenty years younger. He tells me the following story, in a loud voice with a twinge of New York accent as if it's the first time he's ever shared it with me: "I'm ninety-three years old! My wife, Elizabeth, and I met fifty years ago, and she's twenty years younger. I told her she was too young for me. She told me it wasn't true, and that she'd let me know when I got old, and . . ."—he always pauses for the punch line—"she just hasn't let me know yet!" His eyes sparkle as he happily carries his milked coffee to his table, doting over his wife as he sits down. She's a spry seventy-something-year-old. They are in love, and it is ridiculously inspiring and adorable. It's stories like that that make me smile and wonder about our blindness, and being blinded, and seeing the light in love. That make me wonder how love can also make us more ourselves, and more whole.

Love is one of the more interesting lenses through which to examine blind spots: especially falling in love, falling out of love, and first impressions. We are experts at weaving together stories to talk ourselves into or out of things. Falling in love illuminates this: our capacity and penchant for a good story; our complex relationship with passion and its effects;

and all the ways we create meaning and build relationships to fulfill our deep need for connection, acceptance, and whatever that mysterious quality is that drives us to want to merge with and surrender to something greater than ourselves.

In Roman mythology, the god Cupid (son of Venus, goddess of love) was depicted as bringing the whole cosmos into being. If you are struck by his arrow, you can't help yourself—you're falling. It could be your first crush in kindergarten, or a teenage romance, or a relationship that had you stepping right into the mouth of a tiger, totally blind, and in hindsight examining the battle wounds you got from it and exclaiming, "I don't know how I could have done that!"

The fact that love is blind—and blinds us—and is one of the most powerful forces we can experience as humans has been a topic of the centuries: we see what isn't there, and we don't see what is there. Yet we also come to see through the power of love—it's that strong a force. In its best form, it can undo everything we thought about who we are. It can allow us to share our hearts and our whole beings with another person at incredibly deep, vulnerable levels. It can transform our conception of the Divine within ourselves. Love is a paradox: we are blinded by love, and through it we see. Even Cupid himself is often depicted blindfolded!

If mental shortcuts and hidden biases, along with emotions and core beliefs, are subtle causes of blind spots, then love is like a foghorn blowing straight in your ear: not the subtlest blind spot generator in the world. Seeing the blind spots that are connected with first impressions and falling in love brings the fallible human experience into high definition.

Falling in Love

Falling in love with a person helps you fall in love with the world, if you let it. And that love can mature over time. Mature love navigates all levels and stages of feeling and human behavior—not discounting them, but illuminating what they are. It's also true that even if you've been in relationship for many years, you can fall in love all over again.

No one has ever said, "I decided to fall in love with Ramesh yesterday" or "I decided not to fall in love with Cindy yesterday afternoon—it's just not worth it." Or "I decided to love my third child best and have a hard time loving my first." We have little if any control over whom we love. It is automatic—guided and influenced by a myriad of factors. We can't make love happen, and we can't *unmake* it happen. Love can be a product of our fast-thinking system, outside the slow-thinking system's control. It's what we do with that arrow when it—bam!—strikes that matters.

Think of a time when you fell in love fast—and hard. It might have been a new love, or maybe you fell after knowing someone for a year or ten years, but recall that moment when everything changed about your orientation to that person. You probably didn't expect it, and it may have had a feeling of inevitability or destiny, taking over your entire life even for a short period of time. It may or may not have been requited.

Recall the scenario and reflect upon how it felt. Perhaps you couldn't stop thinking about that person. You felt giddy and ridiculously happy and content when you were around them, and you had a seemingly endless source of energy for spending time with them. You were convinced that you had to be with them; it was fated by the gods. Maybe you even lost sleep or your appetite or you were entirely distracted into a fantasy world about what might be as you projected the feeling into the future. This feeling could last for months, and even years; researchers have discovered that the brains of couples who have been married for thirty years and claim to still be in love resemble those of newly in love couples.[1] This is what we think of as "love at first sight," and no wonder we are all so confused about what the heck love is, how to know whether it's "real" or not, what to do with it once you find it, and what to do with yourself when you don't.

Back to that time when you fell, hard. Just why are some connections so strong? What could have been at play? Was it destiny—meeting your soul mate, whatever that means to you? Was it merely a play of chemicals, or your core wounds magnetizing you toward each other? If you lost the love, do you experience regret? If you still have that love, are you afraid of losing it? Has it developed into a different kind of love? Or do you now see it as an experience that has nothing to do with "real" love?

Perhaps you met and married someone you didn't fall in love with in this way. Does that make your connection any less special? Of course not. I know plenty of couples who developed a deep love over time and have tremendous respect and care for one another. Sometimes they are far happier than couples who got together during a quick honeymoon period and discovered that a long-lasting relationship needed more than what a temporary suspension of disbelief and a period of infatuation had to offer.

Being hit by Cupid's arrow is not a prerequisite to pairing and bonding with someone, yet Hollywood culture would certainly say otherwise! For eons people have married for all kinds of practical reasons and the world seems to have gotten by okay. Yet for just as long, people have also fallen in love. This is why falling in love is rife with our wildest hopes and our biggest illusions and blind spots—it's a strong force that tends to overpower. What are we trying to do when we put so many eggs in the basket of passionate love and create so much meaning from our feelings? Should we or shouldn't we, and how do we navigate it all?

There's science behind what happens as we fall in love and what keeps relationships thriving. We will look at what happens in our biology—but primarily I'm interested in this core thing that drives us: our desire for acceptance, love, and wholeness. It isn't just biology and procreation and practicality. And it's also not just karma or divine will or what's in the stars; all of that is storytelling, making sense and meaning of something that is too complex and mysterious to warrant such a simplistic answer.

Let's look at some of our biological influences and biases. Through that lens we may stumble upon something deeper and more mysterious, which is not a place of answers but of questions to be lived: questions that have everything to do with the exploration and expression of our heart's deepest longings through intimate relating with another person, hopefully in increasingly clear-sighted ways.

The Body on Love

When we fall in love, we feel sweaty palms, flushed cheeks, and feelings of passion and anxiety—accompanied by the reward-seeking neurotransmitter dopamine and a rush of cortisol, the stress hormone, mobilizing to help us deal with our plight. And sometimes, plight it is! Interestingly, when cortisol levels rise, serotonin, the neurotransmitter and natural mood stabilizer found primarily in our gut, gets *depleted*. This results in a plethora of preoccupying thoughts, hopes, and fears that are related to infatuation—and now our brains look a little obsessive-compulsive!

On top of that, we experience increases in adrenaline and an important chemical, norepinephrine, that feels good—but also makes us feel infatuated and obsessed. Combined with the motivated energy of adrenaline in our system, it's no wonder so many of us have good "love is blind" stories![2] What a setup for out-of-the-ordinary behavior. And we all have the capacity to undergo this experience—nobody is exempt.

PRACTICE **Love Is Blind Story**

What's your story? Find a close friend and share together: *The time I blindly fell in love the hardest was* _____ . . . Just let yourself share whatever story comes to you. It could have been in seventh grade: *I was blinded by* . . . and *I was made alive by* . . . Notice what you experience as you finish, and listen to your friend's story too.

I once started a new job and within the first few weeks fell in love with someone I met there. It was classic love at first sight. I saw him coming from a hundred yards away, and my heart stopped. It was the most horrible thing. I was single—he was married. I had zero control; even knowing that it was a nonstarter, and not harboring any illusions that it would work out, I still couldn't help myself. But I practiced mindfully being aware of the thoughts and feelings coming and going, and that really helped. It was humbling to observe that I had no control over it. And the feelings finally shifted a few months later. I never mentioned it or tried to make anything happen, and my patience eventually paid off. While nothing on the outside had changed, something in me had changed, and I couldn't have been happier that it had.

This is good news because it means we don't have to be at the mercy of our biology and impulses, even when they are at their strongest. It was the welcoming of the experience—sensing how I felt in my body and the associated emotions and thoughts—that helped me through it, and when it was over it was really *over*, not still something in the periphery of my experience that I was blindly caught up in. Can you see how meeting such an experience without refusing it puts it in the light and helps us see how to navigate it? It's hard to navigate in the dark, when we relegate such experiences to somewhere beneath our conscious awareness. For sure, it's hard to face them head-on but it's wiser in the long run.

Science tells us what our brains look like when we're in love. Biological anthropologist Helen Fisher studied fMRI images of people's brains on romantic love.[3] When people looked at a photo of a person they loved, their brains became active with dopamine, the "feel-good" neurotransmitter, and regions concerned with pleasure, focused attention, and reward lit up. Dopamine is released even when you just have a crush on someone, by the way. Primitive areas of the brain—such as the amygdala and the hippocampus—are involved in romantic love. The catch is that those areas can also remain lit for long periods; it doesn't have to be a flash-and-fade affair. Heightened by skin-to-skin contact, if things get to that point, the hormones oxytocin and vasopressin are also released, which provide feelings of contentment, calmness, security, and bonding (this happens while holding a newborn as well).

The neural correlate to the adage "Love is blind" comes into play here: romance and love *deactivate* the neural pathway responsible for negative emotions, such as fear and social judgment.[4] When we are engaged in falling in love, so say the researchers, "the neural machinery responsible for making critical assessments of other people . . . shuts down." No wonder we do and say things that we can regret later, or that leave us wondering how we could have been so blind. This explains it, at least partially!

I once referred to a love relationship and declared, "My brain just got hijacked." It can feel that way. When some parts of our brain (the pathways for fear, judgment, and assessment of others, which can be useful when getting to know someone) are not accessible, the feel-good hormones run the show. And this could be a leftover from an evolutionary function that told us to stop scanning for danger and stay still long enough to conceive a little one! Fear can be healthy if it's giving us signals that something is "off" in our environment, but we don't have the chance to receive them if our access to those signals is cut off—*unless* we approach our state mindfully, with greater awareness of what is happening in our brains and bodies. If we are blind to it, we can miss it, but if we awaken to it, we can watch the whole thing happening, not get swept up in it, and have the capacity to make better choices.

I think that, over time, we can learn to understand these ebbs and flows of biology and feeling as coming within a larger context and no longer get caught up in them, even if we are fully aware that they seem and feel believable. We can learn to unhook from patterns that draw us to certain kinds of love experiences, and from blind-spot beliefs that keep us running toward something we mistakenly believe might save us from ourselves. We can feel what we feel and hang out with it rather than acting on it or ignoring it in favor of that next dopamine hit. When we make a turn inward and practice truth telling, life gets real because we can no longer escape through our fantasies and projections; the ways we go blind easily illumine themselves. We don't know where that truth telling will lead, and that's partly what causes us to keep it in the dark, but we can start with ourselves and go from there.

Fisher's years of study caused her to posit that romantic love is a *drive* rather than an *emotion*. And indeed, drives—or motivations—feature dopamine, igniting our arousal system around a specific biological need. Drives are associated with a reward, can last longer than emotions, and are difficult to control. Think of thirst (a drive) as opposed to anger (an emotion), which offers more choice in terms of ways to respond. Note: to illuminate what a drive is, just think about how many times a day you reach for your smartphone! New estimates show the average person checks it eighty times a day (every eleven minutes!), twice as often as we guess we do. And that number is far higher for the power users.[5] That is the effect of dopamine—a text came in! Our brain thinks it is a reward, like a payoff from a slot machine. What if I got a new email or someone posted on Instagram? I am driven to check it.

What do drives have to do with blind spots? Quite a lot. Drives are under the surface and automatic, and we have little control over them. They are easy to miss even though they are in plain sight; they're also hard to shift, because the dopamine response in the brain is so darn compelling. But knowing that you have them and how they show up for you is an important step in bringing an intelligent, conscious awareness to what motivates you, and just might help you make wiser and more informed decisions. Remember that we can migrate wise behaviors from slow to fast thinking? By seeing what is happening in our brains and bodies when we fall in love, we can recognize that more is at play than Cupid's arrow pinging us from above. We can unhook the dreamy, starry-eyed response if we see it for what it is, especially if we are in a relationship or a situation like the one I described about myself, where it's inappropriate to act upon it.

I've seen so many people (and I bet you have too) act upon those feelings in bizarre and uncharacteristic ways—those are examples of going blind and acting out what you don't see. But even if we are falling in love and all the circumstances seem to line up to support it, we can still slow down and engage the part of our brain that likes to shut off in these moments (our judgment and fear centers) to make wiser, more aligned decisions for love in our lives and limit the suffering we experience down the road because we made decisions out of blindness.

We have all (I'll speak for myself) gone "wrong" in love, gone blind and made mistakes because our first impressions were wildly inaccurate. I've heard myself saying out loud spontaneously after dating someone, "How the heck did I miss that?" It hurts to be so off in our judgment, yet that is how we learn. It's humbling; it shows us how much we don't know that we thought we did. Especially in the realm of dating and love.

Help, I'm Falling!

If you're in the throes of a new attraction, here is the practice for you. Note: This is not a sit-for-a-bit-and-contemplate practice. This is a make-choices-in-real-time practice, repeated over time until you can see with greater clarity.

1 *Slow down.* Pause: do not act on your feelings right away. Give yourself time to get to know how it is to be with this person. If it's a keeper, the relationship will still be there several months from now and you will thank yourself for slowly living into it.

2 Ask yourself: *Are there assumptions I'm making because of how I'm feeling swept away? If I let myself know what I know about this person, and admit it, what do I see?*

Mindfulness in Love

Did you know that we weight intense experiences more heavily and overlook smaller experiences over time?[6] That's why, if a work or love relationship ends poorly, we tend to judge the whole thing as bad. But what if we learn to weight each moment equally?

What if you had access to a quality of moment to moment well-being that considered the highs and lows of life and helped you appreciate the profoundly precious nature of *each* moment—not blindly overvaluing one moment that happened two years ago or, conversely, blindly under-valuing a five-year-long series of moments you shared with a parent or a friend? Perhaps if you allowed for the full spectrum, your friendships, love relationships, and work relationships could weather a little more storm. This is the long view, of course, and it's easy to forget. Pigeonholing people is the easy route. The more difficult one requires an effort to bring conscious awareness to each fresh, new moment, learning from your mistakes. Remembering the past, of course, but also being willing to meet the present, aware of your biases and ready to act in a responsive rather than reactive way. Imagine falling fully in love *without* an agenda and *with* conscious awareness, and the impact that could have on you.

You feel more and you know more—a great combination. Then every moment would be a chance to fall in love, repeatedly.

Cheating and Truth Telling

One reason I feel interested in illuminating going blind in love is that I've been cheated on. And it sucks. I wish my ex had known a thing or two about what was happening in his brain and body, and had been willing to speak the truth before it ever got to the point where he lived out (and hid) a second relationship. If he had revealed the truth, we both could have chosen what to do about it. But instead, what happened was a clusterf*ck of a situation that caused an immense amount of pain, confusion, and suffering.

One more note here! Even when human beings do crazy things to each other, such as cheat or lie or be deceptive, they are still trying to do one thing: get their needs for acceptance, love, and connection met. Often when people go about it in these unhealthy or unproductive ways, they are acting out to try to create what they may have *never felt* in their entire lives. But guess what: they won't get it in a lasting way by doing stuff like having an affair; that's just not how that works—it has to be an inside job. The good news is that in going all the way into what drives us and seeing it, we can find our path to something far deeper and truer in the quality of connection we are looking for. We are hurt relationally and we also heal relationally, and the number-one relationship we are healing is the one with ourselves.

So how do we sort all this out? Fisher separates the whole falling-in-love process into three parts: lust, attraction, and attachment.[7] We can be in a long-term relationship with someone we love (attachment) while simultaneously being attracted sexually (lust) to any number of people, and even experience falling in love (attraction) at the same time. Knowing some of the science behind what our brain is doing and the behavioral research across cultures and animal species doesn't have to take the mystery and specialness out of connecting with, marrying, partnering up with, or dating someone. And it doesn't mean we become rudderless and throw our ethics and morals out the window—it's quite the opposite. It can be helpful to illuminate and understand these processes so we don't fall into blind, patterned reactivity when we *do* feel some of these things. Normalizing what is happening in our biology is a powerful tool to harness our own awareness and inspire behaving with integrity despite our bodies going wild, or more likely, the *fear* of our bodies going wild, especially when we're in long-term relationships.

We make many of the bad choices regarding these sorts of scenarios because we are afraid to speak the truth to ourselves or our partner. We fear we may lose something if we do. We have an idea that we are not allowed to have these feelings, so when they come up we relegate them to the unconscious and act them out or cut ourselves off from our own truth. We create distance internally as we struggle against what we think we shouldn't feel. Or we create distance externally from those we love the most, which can enable the whole drama to build on itself and become way bigger than it ever needed to be. That truth may lie in a situation like this: *I feel disconnected. I'm not getting some significant needs met. I want to explore this together, even though I find myself starting to look outside our marriage for these things.* Or *I'm finding myself attracted to someone and I don't want to act that out unconsciously. I want to share it with you and talk about it so we can approach this situation together as a supportive team.* I've seen it so many times: People cheat because they are scared to lose their partner if they say the truth, that they aren't feeling connected anymore. Or they do it because they are out of touch with what is going on in their bodies and minds and are hence driven by their unconscious drives to gain acceptance from outside themselves, taking those drives to be the "truth" and creating scenarios to try to get those needs met. Either way, they are in hiding and acting from a blind spot.

There is another way! Telling the truth creates rather than destroys intimacy, if it's told in an authentic relationship. That authenticity helps me feel safe to speak the truth, and I wonder: could that be true for you too, if you concluded that the truth brings light and can heal what is awry? Even when it's hard or may cause you to lose something you hold dear, or at least have to face the fear of that loss?

We cling to "shoulds" to stay safe and protect ourselves. But at what cost? I'd rather be committed to the truth (what is alive and real) than to something I've been told I should do (an imposition from the outside that won't stand up under pressure). Truth is alive and real, and holds the seeds of an inner guidance that is ethical and kind to ourselves and others. You can trust it too. If you commit to truth together with someone, you know that they aren't committing to you out of hiddenness and fear but straight from the heart because they love the truth too. And that truth can be rooted in an ideal of commitment. But if you're in a relationship where someone else doesn't answer with truth or is unable to hear yours, that doesn't mean you should put a muzzle on or tiptoe around them. That's not fair to either of you. At the same time, there's no need to blast someone with the truth. Truth in love can be soft, and firm.

What about those who cheat on their partners but still claim to love them? Fisher's work shows that it's possible to feel both forms of love simultaneously, but that begs a question: What is love? What does that word even mean? Some of us, married or single, go chasing it all over creation, especially if we don't feel whole inside. Yet love is so much more than the search for completeness; it's the expression of completeness. It goes back to that adage *What you seek is seeking you*. Love is already whole and our quest to find it can get in the way of our seeing that it is already here and fulfilled within us.

Halo or Horns

Another key way we go blind in love, and life, is through first impressions. We tend to trust our intuition and judgment at the first split-second moment. But what happens during a first impression? Well, all sorts of unconscious processes are occurring: in the blink of an (attentive) eye we evaluate friend, foe, mate, or lunch. In the wild we didn't have time to make a list and check it twice; we needed to be able to see clear as day whether someone was hunting us, we were hunting them, or they were a potential mate. And that lightning-quick judgment we make gets confirmed by our slower, more rational system: since we just thought it up so quickly and so certainly, it must be real! We aren't the greatest at checking our own intuitions, as we have seen, and we tend to believe, despite evidence to the contrary, that our intuitions are correct (remember confirmation bias?). Why is that? We have a few interesting filters that lead us to be completely blind as we generate a first impression about anyone—not just a love interest. It has a fancy name, coined by Daniel Kahneman, called *the illusion of validity*. Don't worry: you're not the only one who does it. Even experts do.[8]

Say you're in a bad mood one day because you didn't get enough sleep and you don't feel too great. You have a work meeting with a potential marketing partner for the first time and immediately decide you don't like the guy. And you think it's because of *him*. But you don't realize that all these other factors that have nothing to do with him have contributed to your flash judgment, not to mention the way he looks or the environment you meet him in, or the way he reminds you of your cousin or your former lover. I mean, from the research experiments I've seen, I wouldn't be surprised if something as simple as stroking velvet versus Velcro before you walk in the room would make you like a person as opposed to feeling they are prickly. That's how susceptible we are to a much larger environment of causation.

One of the cognitive mistakes we make when meeting someone for the first time is called *the halo effect*, named by psychologist Edward Thorndike in the early twentieth century to describe how we allow our overall impression of someone to color how we view their character.[9] Without knowing it, we tend to make people *all* good (halo) or *all* bad (I call it the "horn" effect—the devil's headwear) based on how we feel when we first meet them. Part of the reason for this is that we are basing our judgments on small pieces of information ("thin slicing," as Malcolm Gladwell calls it), and then extrapolating that out to make the best coherent story we can. It's what our brains do to fill in gaps of information; we make ginormous assumptions and completely miss the fact that we are doing so because it feels so *right*. Of course, sometimes it is right. But it's a filter that sometimes helps us go wrong.

I was recently working on a group project designing a mindfulness training that was to have massive social impact, and all our hearts were fully invested in a great outcome. We kicked off the project with a dinner. Immediately I formed first impressions of everyone I hadn't already known at the table. Since my intuition feels right-on most of the time,

I naturally trusted what I instinctively judged: this person is creative and professional and will play together well on the team, that person doesn't listen well and won't have much to contribute, this person is a bit unstable, that person is going to be an amazing pinch hitter.

Want to know my accuracy? It was dismal. I couldn't have been more wrong about my first impressions, compared to what I discovered over time. Yet at other times, since my intuition had been correct, I naturally trusted what first came to mind. This backs up what Daniel Kahneman discovered and has been suggested in other studies as well, from the NBA to military drafting. In one such experiment, Israeli army experts formed first impressions of new recruits during a group exercise and judged which ones would be the best leaders. There was no correlation between who those experts had predicted to be the best leaders and what happened in the field over time.[10]

People are very good at assuming—even faced with data that proves otherwise, like being told that their first impressions are not accurate—that *they* are the exception to the rule. Our intuitions and judgments feel so real because they are right there in front of us. Mix that together with availability, hindsight, and confirmation bias and you've got quite a cocktail of ways in which to fool and blind yourself. Then we do something else fun that tops it all off! We ignore our own errors by not factoring in our own ignorance.[11] It is this combination—and more—of intuitive mistakes that cause us to be blind when we first meet someone.

Don't worry: we will get to how our intuition *works for us* later in the book. It can be an exquisitely fine-tuned machine and is a primary guidance system for our navigation of life. There are times when our first impressions are spot-on. Here I'm highlighting where it can go wrong and send us off track.

For example, say you meet someone, judge them as one of the most wonderful human beings you've ever met, and fall in love with them, enjoying an amazing few weeks of romance and happiness. Then over the next five months they prove consistently that their behavior is self-serving, abusive to others, and unkind to the world around them. Have you ever dated or worked for someone like that? We increase the weight of our first impression, and subsequent information gets filtered through the original emotional response to them, which is why it sometimes doesn't compute that they could hurt us. "But they're so wonderful! How could they do that?" We *suppress* ambiguity and *exaggerate* emotional coherence to keep our story going and not question it, and in doing so hurt ourselves by not admitting the truth.[12] *That* is the kind of life lesson we receive when we unearth a big blind spot like that, and it will tame our idea that what we see in a first impression is trustworthy.

My saying this won't do too much to tame it, but life has a way of letting us see the fallacy of our own ideas. When you are aware of the halo effect, you can judge someone at first impression in a balanced way because you are more likely to consider the whole person. This doesn't have to make you wary about meeting people and trusting humanity's basic goodness or your own intuition, but it can make you more balanced and aware, and in the future less disappointed or surprised when certain aspects of a person's personality and life emerge that may contradict your original one-sided belief.

Wild Cards

We continually surprise each other, and ourselves. We are all wild cards at heart; we have the potential to do any given thing in any given moment—don't we? We just can't help it: we are complex, dynamic, emergent processes that learn and change and adapt to new environments. When we have a first impression that someone is a jerk and they end up being a kind person, it doesn't fit into our original—and strongly held—belief, so we can even end up *dis*believing the facts; confirmation bias helps us keep our previously formed opinion in place by ignoring relevant information. Or conversely, we may be so shocked by someone's inappropriate behavior after a positive assessment of their character that we remain in shock and the news that there are red flags doesn't get all the way in. This is how you can walk into the lion's mouth of a bad relationship—and stay in it for years—even as your friends lament that you are ignoring important warning signs. The bad stuff doesn't compute so it gets left out of the equation! How simple we are as sorting and processing machines!

Here are some questions we may blindly ask when we're surprised by someone's behavior after a flash judgment of halo (*They're wonderful!*) or horn (*Run away*):

- Initial judgment: halo—we are gullible and ostrich-like when they behave in a negative way: *Why would he be so mean (or incompetent)?*

- Initial judgment: horn—we are mistrustful when they behave in a positive way: *What do they want from me?* or *Why are they acting so nice?*

Thoughts like these are signs that you have been struck by halo or horn first impressions. You've got to allow ambiguity and a little room for the gray areas in life—because they are there regardless! Letting in the truth will help you take wiser, more aligned steps to navigate relational nuances. And there's that good old thing called truth telling too: We hide the truth from ourselves, don't we? I've always been so curious about the ways we do that, sticking our heads in the sand.

We don't need to be either Pollyannas or complete skeptics; the truth lies somewhere in the middle. The darn middle! We are not wired to orient to the middle. Our brains are wired for survival and to see what's novel—on either end of the spectrum—and then try to analyze it with an incredibly small amount of data. That's why slowing down while moving through life and knowing you don't know while acknowledging what you *do* know are so freaking important. If we don't, we are driven by our fast-thinking system that, rightfully so, jumps to conclusions—and occasionally jumps right into the fire.

All you need to do—especially if you are falling in love, but in any first-impression situation—is ask, "Is there something I'm not seeing?" That question alone will evoke what is true—*of course* there *is* something you're not seeing—and holding that in your awareness can lead you to be more open and honest to what is there, and what is true. It helps you slow down. And it leads to less judgment because you see that you have all aspects of good and bad within yourself. When you know that you can be a total jerk sometimes even though you are kind most of the time, you can make space for others to do the same. Then life gets more interesting. There's so much about *you* that you don't know. And there's so much about *me* that I don't know. *Bless our hearts.*

•

To round out this chapter, let's zoom out from looking at love between two people, and look at love in the wider world in which we live.

Blind Spots and Love for the World

Sometimes it's easier to put your head in the sand, ignore the evening news, and stay in your happy little life bubble. Life in the wider world can be overwhelming. You might say to yourself, *If I'm having a hard time with my job and neighbors, how can I let in all the suffering happening across the globe? It's unfair to myself to take on that responsibility, and I don't have enough love to go around!* It's easy to go blind to large-scale suffering and not know how to share love toward the many challenged communities around the globe. There is an antidote to our blindness to mass suffering, though, that isn't draining and that doesn't require more than you can give. It's called altruism.

Altruism means acting with unselfish concern for the welfare of others, and is a form of love that goes far beyond concern for self and close family, reaching people we may never know and may not necessarily like, let alone love. Altruism is what happens when you jump into harm's way in order to save a stranger; it's what motivated some people to run toward the twin towers in New York City during the 9/11 attacks rather than away. It's what happens when you are motivated, with an energy that surprises you, to bring cookies to a neighbor or sign up to spend your vacation helping kids with dental needs in Africa. It comes from a different place—a selfless place—and doesn't take a toll on you but rather is deeply fulfilling. Altruism may be what gets someone into signing up to work with the United Nations to help refugees who are living in camps because of mass relocation from war or famine.

I have traveled to the Middle East as part of the teaching staff on a program managed by the United Nations Foundation to teach mindfulness and self-compassion to humanitarian personnel who are stressed and fatigued from working tirelessly with the victims of war. Although they may have signed up for their work from an altruistic place, sometimes the situation can get quite stressful and they need support to find the replenishment and purpose that will enable them to step back into the fray. I went to Jordan and taught a practice to humanitarian workers servicing the needs of the more than five hundred thousand Syrian refugees in the country. You can do this practice too, to reinvigorate a sense of connection with the whole globe, one person at a time.

PRACTICE   **Just Like Me**

I learned this simple yet powerful practice, called Just Like Me, from Meng at Google. Applying it in Jordan, all the participants there, many of whom worked in high-stakes environments, sat facing each other in pairs as I read a list of phrases:

- This person has wants and needs, just like me.

- This person has felt hurt, just like me.

- This person wants to be loved, just like me.

We also listed the ways we wished for the other person's happiness and well-being, such as "I wish you to be free from suffering," or "I wish you to have healthy and supportive relationships." The group was diverse, including people of different religions—Muslims, Jews, and Christians. Regardless of race, religion, or gender, these people sat together and received the person across from them with a tenderness and love that is rarely witnessed in our everyday lives. When we ended there were many hugs, and tears shed, from the power of a few short minutes of being with another person in this way.

This practice, the participants shared, required nothing of them other than a natural well-wishing for the welfare of others. They could let go of the responsibility they had come to shoulder, for all of the pressing needs and requests of the large refugee community, and instead simply meet them at this basic human level where they could see similarities and wish the best for each other without giving up too much of their own self-care and self-kindness. It felt more equal and realistic than being on the hook to save everyone, something they would never be able to accomplish.

I heartily challenge anyone who belittles the power of kindness, compassion, self-awareness, and insight, and the slow work of the heart and of bringing shadow into light. These qualities will save our world and save us from ourselves. We do the work with ourselves first, and then bring it outward into our families and communities.

We need healing so desperately on this planet and it's our job to listen, to love, to lean in, and to accept what—and who—is around us. The more of us who can train ourselves to lean toward being undefended, open, and compassionate, the closer we get to a better world. This gets especially tricky considering all of our hidden biases about race and religion, and how we instinctively lack empathy for people who look different from us and can end up fearing whole races of people because of cultural biases, media, and the beliefs our communities hold:[13] "Oooh, there's a young black man with a hoodie on—he must be dangerous" or "Is that person wearing a hijab? Maybe she's a terrorist." We don't intend to think those things, but if we are willing to look and be honest with ourselves, we will find them lying beneath the radar of our conscious experience. How do we not only get beyond bias, but also care for our world and have empathy for the suffering around us?

I spoke with Ruth King, an African American meditation teacher and author of *Mindful of Race*, about the issues of racial division in the United States. She shared that it's important to get to know your own race's beliefs and blind spots before you try to bridge a gap between races or create racial healing. Her suggestion is for white people in the United States to "own" their whiteness, see their difference, and understand what it is to identify with a group of people (white) rather than being an individual. Identifying with and understanding ourselves as members of a group and knowing its associated privilege, challenges, and history will change our world, she says, because we can then take responsibility as a group of people and respond to the messes we as a group have caused. She points out that black people in the United States don't have a choice—they are immediately identified as a "group"—while white people see themselves as individuals and have a choice whether to identify as a group, and therein lies the privilege.

If we jump too quickly to look through a "color blind" lens, we will miss out on these kinds of blind spots and on a more nuanced understanding of the underlying causes and conditions of where we find ourselves today, no matter our race, religion, or sexual preference. We have to see through the lens of color and difference in order to undo our hidden biases, and ultimately to see all the way through to our interconnectedness and similarities, as we did in the Just Like Me practice.

The heart of suffering and the heart of our blind spots originate when we take ourselves to be isolated, separate, limited, and lacking: *I'm alone, I'm not connected, I am not free, and I need to know, do, or be something to be complete.* Division, confusion, struggle, and conflict are all rooted in this basic blind spot.

What I have discovered, and am still recognizing, is that there is a fundamental quality of wholeness in community, rooted in belonging; it is interconnected, free, and fulfilled just as it is. It's the viewpoint of wholeness, not the viewpoint of confusion and division, that helps you to know this.

Wholeness in community can happen when we have found wholeness in ourselves. If this feels like a pie-in-the-sky concept, check it out for yourself: During any of your worst moments, or when you are stuck in a difficult emotion or pain in your body, is there something that welcomes and accepts that moment just as it is in your experience? Even if the part of you that recognizes this is only a drop in the ocean of your suffering, can you tune in to that part that is not resisting this moment? And if you can't, ask: Is there something here that is rested, that sits with what comes nonjudgmentally, and that *loves what is* right now? Some aspect of yourself that isn't pushing back on life? Find out what is real—for *you*. This isn't a religious philosophy or an ideology.

It's a lived experience. To witness your own suffering from a place of radical welcoming helps you recognize this in a deep and authentic way, closing divisions. When you stop refusing one part of yourself, you will stop refusing one part of your community. Loving from wholeness eases suffering because you let go of resistance, and in that letting go, your birthright is a natural, spontaneous, wise, deeply kind responsiveness to each and every moment that comes your way. We have access to all parts of ourselves, including what we have not yet encountered, and we trust that in seeing the whole, we—and the world—are better for it.

●

I'll close this chapter with three practices to illuminate some of the aspects of love we have explored here.

PRACTICE   Discovering Truth

Take a moment and sit quietly. Reflect on how you may hold your truth back: from yourself, or from your partner if you are in relationship. Or reflect on how you impose your ideas on yourself or your partner to gain security. Notice what comes to you, and allow it with a quality of welcoming and presence. Ask: *Where do I hold my truth back with myself or my partner? Where do I impose my ideas on myself or partner? What would a deeper surrender to what is most true and most alive look like for me right now?* Simply notice what you discover.

PRACTICE   Loving from Wholeness

Take a moment and do the Five Mindful Breaths practice (see chapter 1, page 17). Center yourself and then open your attention. Notice the environment around you, as well as your inner environment. See if you can access that part of yourself that holds and welcomes all of who you are: your wholeness. It may be a part of you that is not resisting anything in your experience. Even if it's a tiny part of you, just notice what it is like to be with the whole of life: your pain, your joy, your hopes and fears, without resistance. Exactly as they are. Rest here in this quality of welcoming presence to your one wild and precious life. Come close to yourself—the full spectrum of you. This is loving from wholeness. Know that you can meet any pain or difficulty from this place of rest and openness.

PRACTICE   Just Like Me, Extended

Sit facing another person. Then repeat the following phrases, while looking at your partner. You can choose to do this silently or aloud.

- This person has a body and a mind, just like me.

- This person has feelings, emotions, and thoughts, just like me.

- This person has, in his or her life, experienced physical and emotional pain and suffering, just like me.

- This person has at some point been sad, disappointed, angry, or hurt, just like me.

- This person has felt unworthy or inadequate, just like me.

- This person wishes to be free from pain and suffering, just like me.

- This person wishes to be safe and healthy, just like me.

- This person wishes to be happy, just like me.

- This person wishes to be loved, just like me.

Now, allow some wishes for well-being to arise, again either silently or aloud, as you choose.

- I wish that this person have the strength, resources, and social support to navigate the difficulties in life with ease.

- I wish that this person be free from pain and suffering.

- I wish that this person be peaceful and happy.

- I wish that this person be loved.

- Because this person is a fellow human being, just like me.

7

SELF-COMPASSION . . .
AND THE BIG REVEAL

What happens when people open their hearts? . . .
They get better.

HARUKI MURAKAMI, *Norwegian Wood*[1]

A FEW YEARS AGO, Roberto, a student in a yoga and meditation class I taught at San Quentin State Prison with James Fox of the Prison Yoga Project, described how it felt to go up for parole and face the families of his victims. He had, before age twenty, along with another person, killed a man and injured another in an attempted car burglary that turned violent. He had since spent almost thirty years behind bars doing transformative inner work, including ten years of yoga and emotional intelligence training. He's a poster child for the rehabilitation movement within the California Department of Corrections and Rehabilitation. Typically, CDCR forgets the "R" part of its name—most inmates are left to fend for themselves—but Roberto lucked out when he was assigned to live in a prison that is served by 70 percent of the prison volunteers in the state of California. It doesn't hurt that he is receptive to learning and to taking responsibility, or that he has gleaned from his life experiences the hard-won qualities of earnestness and wisdom.

Suffice it to say, Roberto was an ideal candidate for parole. As he shared his story about the parole hearing, I could hear the compassion with which he described the scene—the pain of the victim's families, who had repeatedly blocked his release, the stone-faced panel of judges, and his own discomfort with and shame about the situation. It was painful all around. "All I can do is be myself up there," he told me, "feel how overwhelming it is, and show up the best I know how. I know I've changed, and I try to display that, despite how intimidating it is to be there."

It's of primary importance that all of us, like Roberto, learn to be kind to ourselves as a starting point as we develop the emotional intelligence it takes to uncover our blind spots. This is self-compassion in action—*showing up the best that we know how*. Being willing to be seen and to care for ourselves and those around us. Considering a situation clearly by seeing it from all sides, and having the willingness to step into it just as we are and face what comes. We can only embrace challenging situations in which our vulnerabilities or faults may be exposed if the willingness to meet our real selves, in each moment, is part of our fundamental orientation to learning and growth. Curiosity and openness are qualities that lie at the heart of developing emotional intelligence, and if we don't have them, our growth will likely be stymied.

Since Roberto was paroled, I've been fortunate to meet up with him a few times. Even on "the outside," you rarely find people with his incredible presence, curiosity, and attentiveness, and the care with which he moves through the world. He's fortunate, and he knows it, and he describes himself as living every day with tremendous gratitude. Now *that* is freedom.

It takes courage to be like Roberto, vulnerable, facing life on its own terms with an open, compassionate heart. When we meet our shadow and kindly tell ourselves the truth, we more easily uncover hidden aspects of ourselves and the links between them and our behaviors, emotions, and judgments. It is exactly when we start to see from this more well-rounded place all that is lurking in the out-of-the-way places in our psyche that we most need self-compassion. If we can be kind to ourselves and hang out with what we discover for long enough, we will also encounter the gifts and messages that have been longing for revelation and airtime.

Compassionate Unmasking

Your particular blind spots don't have to have the massive implications that Roberto's did. Yours could be as simple as coming to grips with the fact that your desire to be liked—something most of us want—has been driving everything you do. As a result, you're never really just being yourself but are instead always chasing after an idealized self-image to present to the world. (This is actually a common blind spot, by the way.) Just think of the billions of photos uploaded to Instagram and Facebook of happy, smiling people with margaritas in their hands at the beach or a restaurant, or with arms wrapped around their partner or kids. Each of us has been there, and we know all too well that the snapshot came sometime before or after (or during) a challenging moment: a feeling of disconnect or of not looking our best (or anywhere close to it). What about the photos we *didn't* upload because we look like a bloated alien or like we haven't slept in a week?

It is exhausting to chase after an image to present to the world, and ultimately, it doesn't meet your underlying need for acceptance. It's like a hungry ghost that is never satisfied, no matter how many "likes" you receive on social media. In facing a blind spot such as realizing that wanting to be liked drives everything you do, you get the first glimmer that you don't really *know how* to be your genuine self, without any masks. What a realization! But how do you unmask without feeling like you are standing there naked for everyone to see? And what might you find? What if your genuine unmasked self isn't enough and you'll lose friends—those people who "like" you?

The only way to truly unmask is to do so with compassion. Following is an exercise to help you get some practice in this.

PRACTICE   Compassionate Unmasking

- Stand in front of a mirror. This can be a physical mirror or a metaphoric one, where you simply reflect upon yourself.

- Strip away the layers of images you hold about yourself and how you should be, along with the roles you play in the world: sister, mother, wife, manager, or any other category you may normally place yourself into.

- When you do so, what is left? *This is your genuine, unmasked self.*

- See and hold yourself in the light of your own compassionate gaze. Nobody else needs to know that you're doing it. Unmasking with compassion helps you discover what is at the core, or essence, of who you are. It doesn't exclude the many roles and social masks you wear. Rather, it includes them but is not *defined by* them.

- Meet yourself anew in this way: see yourself deeply for who you are at your essence. When you practice doing so, you can use this way of meeting yourself unmasked as an anchor for those times when you wish you were somehow other than you are. Seeing yourself as you are, without roles or judgments, is deeply loving and compassionate. It's what we ask the world to reflect to us: our worthiness and value. In this practice we give that to ourselves first, at a foundational level: we are gracious toward what we see and experience.

To make this a little more concrete, here are a few insights you could potentially discover through compassionately unmasking the ways you behave in order to be liked.

1 In order to be liked, I please others by doing what I think they think I should do. In this way I am out of touch with what I really want and who I really am.

2 In order to be liked, I refuse to listen to feedback that conflicts with my idealized self-image. My way of coping is to blame others for their "false" images of me, which could never be true. In this way I am out of touch with the "full catastrophe" of who I am, and people end up disliking me for shaming them. That is the opposite of what I want.

3 In order to be liked, I avoid taking risks because I am afraid people will reject me. By staying small I stay liked, but I don't like myself and I don't get to have the adventures I want in life.

Seeing through this blind spot and its impact on our lives may bring up emotions such as guilt or shame. When we see that most things we do are driven by an unfulfilled need for acceptance, we think, *I'm a fraud!* These patterned ways of moving through the world are hard to let go of, and we can fear we'll be judged by others if we show up in new and different ways from how we've always been seen. This is where self-compassion comes in: it helps us look at those feelings of guilt or shame and see how natural they are, and that most of us share them. Those images we've been creating and trying to live up to have helped us stay safe to an extent, but it's time to let them go by letting them in, with kindness. That is how we can discover their message—their gift—and learn how to act on it in our lives.

It may not seem like a gift, at first, to discover that after all these years of trying to be who you think you should be, you don't really know how to be authentically you. But it is actually a wonderful opportunity to find connection with your essential nature—what makes you *you*—and to open to the exploration of removing the masks that *aren't you* in social situations. It's through trial and error that you discover this, because there is no bull's-eye "perfectly authentic" way to be. Ultimately there is no error, or trial—it's really all an experiment, one best conducted with tender compassion. A mentor of mine once told me, when I was comparing myself to him, "How about you do Kelly and I'll do me. Do Kelly really well—go all the way with it." Nice life advice! I'm still working on it.

Easing Defensiveness

Realizing stuff about ourselves and then balancing it out with compassion helps us find flow and ease in life. It's like a continual conversation between sudden, often uncomfortable epiphanies and a kind and gentle embrace. But sometimes compassion toward ourselves can't flow naturally because our inner judgment continues to dominate. We harbor an idea that how we are isn't okay, or feel guilty for causing others pain (perhaps, for example, in our blindness we've been judgmental and critical toward our partner) and wham! Self-compassion takes a hike.

For example, has someone ever told you that you hurt them, and you felt so defensive that you couldn't even hear what they were saying? Or have you ever tried to tell another person—a partner, a parent, a coworker—that you felt hurt when they spoke to you in a certain tone or when they dismissed your creative suggestion, and all they did was defend themselves, explain it away, and then attack you for "blaming" them? One person tries to express hurt or pain and the other gets defensive and lashes out in response. I think I can safely say we have all been in that situation (and on both sides of it).

If we're the defended one in this scenario and we recognize we're feeling that defensiveness, we can extend compassion to the places within us that feel under "attack." Then we'll actually have space to hear that we impacted someone else without making it a personal affront and defending a false (because it's perfect) image of ourselves at all costs.

As we learn to do this—and we *can* learn, through practice—we realize that self-compassion opens up space for others, with their pain included. We can still have opinions, and still listen with discriminative wisdom, but we don't feel threatened by someone else's feelings. With this in mind, you can see that it's not selfish to meet yourself deeply and love all of who you are (including the parts that feel unlovable!). In fact, it's probably the best thing you can do to be a kinder and more understanding human being in the world.

Authentic Self-Compassion

Before we begin to ask others to help reveal our blind spots (the subject of the next chapter), we need to examine our own vulnerability and learn how to develop key resources like self-kindness that allow us to stay with the challenge of hearing something that is hard to hear or seeing something that is hard to see. Looking through the lens of self-compassion, we find the aspects of power and truth within our vulnerabilities that will guide us in bringing blind spots into the light.

Full disclosure: I used to dislike the idea of "cultivating self-compassion." It seemed half selfish, half dorky, and full-on navel-gazey. I thought you either had compassion or you didn't, and trying to cultivate it was a way to fake yourself out, being nice to yourself in an inauthentic way. *I'm so awesome! Really, I love myself! It's all good!* But sometimes we feel plain old shitty, so why not admit the truth?

In that spirit, enter the phrase "embrace the suck." It's an expression some military veterans I've worked with use to help each other get through the tough times of deployment and battle. Go with what is hard and push through it rather than trying to overcome difficulties with platitudes. I agree with my veteran students that the only way to handle something hard is to go through it, not around it. You can't bypass a difficult truth just by trying to be nice to yourself and telling yourself it's all good.

But I was wrong about self-compassion. What *isn't* kind about mindfully giving yourself a pause, getting in touch with a sense of well-being, meeting challenging emotions and life experiences, and welcoming yourself as you are, warts and all? That is being mindful with your vulnerability . . . and that is self-compassion. It doesn't have to be packaged in the obvious language of some of the traditional self-compassion practices you may have heard of, like repeating, "May I be at peace," but it's still at the heart of all this work. Just as the space in the room doesn't refuse our being in it, there is part of our natural experience that doesn't refuse who and how we are. Getting in touch with this part of us is self-compassion, and will serve us well as we peer into the recesses of our blessed little psyches. This is essential if we are to look at our blind spots and the challenging, hurt, and sometimes frightening parts of ourselves. Otherwise it's tough to have the bandwidth to hang out with what is hard long enough to get to the other side of it.

Now let's take a break from this discussion and get in a little self-compassion practice.

Take a moment to connect with whatever is alive in your experience right now. Notice what that is: a feeling, an emotion, a sound in your environment, or the feeling of contact with the surface you're sitting on. Now pause, and see if you can also get in touch with a quality of ease and well-being.

If this doesn't come easily to you, imagine yourself on a warm, sunny summer afternoon, resting in a hammock with a glass of lemonade in your hand. You have turned off your smartphone—in fact, you've left it inside the house. There is nothing you need to do and nowhere you have to be. That kind of ease.

Or perhaps another image arises: you are with trusted family enjoying a relaxing Sunday afternoon, or you're in your favorite place outdoors, in nature, able to be yourself fully and rest.

This moment of ease, while allowing your experience to be just as it is, is the simple ongoing work of mindfulness—and it can't be underestimated. Feeling safe and at ease is a necessary ingredient in the recipe for natural self-compassion. Rest for a few moments here in this sense of well-being and notice it as a felt sense in your whole body.

Can you see how this kind, supportive moment is already there—and you're just joining with it? This moment has been resting all along in a place of natural compassion toward yourself and all of life.

Now, if it feels right, place a hand on your heart and sense love and compassion toward yourself, for how you are and how you feel right now, in this moment. Notice what you discover.

Carry this discovery into whatever you plan to do next.

If you return to this natural self-compassion practice again and again in ordinary moments, it will become an instinctive response you can call upon when the going gets tough. You can do it when you're standing in line at the grocery store. Notice all the tension you're holding in your body and how your mind is racing, or distracted by the news on your smartphone—and then hit that imaginary hammock. Practice when you have a moment to hang out on your couch or are falling asleep. Just allow a little space for kindness in your felt experience: it's that simple. All those little moments of practice add up and can contribute to a new set point of self-compassion that will help you tremendously as you navigate your life and face your blind spots honestly.

Self-Compassion When You Don't Feel Like It

As I touched on before, compassion practice—pausing and giving others and yourself a little TLC—is often taught formally using traditional phrases like "May you be happy" or "May I be at peace." But when things don't seem to be going well, and we can't instantly access a sense of kindness and caring for others or ourselves, this can feel uncomfortable, or even distressing. That's when we start judging ourselves for not doing compassion practice "right." It's hard to access compassion and kindness when what we are actually feeling is depression, confusion, or boredom. Or maybe we're feeling pissed off at our partner, or someone else. Like all good practices, self-compassion can backfire on us if it isn't authentic in the moment, and then it won't work. But when you "fail" at it, that's when it gets really juicy. It's a gift, because it helps you come back to what is *really* here and meet *that* on its own terms. Which is actually success, and not failure at all.

So, for example, pause when your young children are fighting, and rather than reacting, allow a moment of grace for yourself and for them; see how it's tough to be a kid and to have to share your mom's attention and your toys, and it's tough to be a mom and have to referee all of these fights. And guess what. That is compassion in action! You don't have to sit and think, *I love myself and I wish for all people everywhere to be happy* or *I wish for my children to be at peace*, although those are wonderful phrases to practice and can help tremendously. But I've seen people repeat these serene phrases in lotus pose in yoga class and then rush out the door and cut somebody off while blasting out of the parking lot. So we need to bring compassion to *both* intentional practice and life as we encounter it, by meeting our experience on its own terms and loving ourselves through it all, with a quality of willingness and attentiveness. This is the wisest way to navigate being human. And it can become automatic when we understand this through insight and practice over time. We find our inner and outer judgment softening naturally.

Softening Judgment

Why is this softening so essential when working with blind spots? Because it is our inner judgment that hardens us and keeps us from seeing clearly. Softening judgment loosens our fight, flight, or freeze threat response—which is often held subconsciously in our nervous systems—by helping us meet and welcome our underlying need for safety and avoidance of blame. When we see clearly, it's easier to have space to hang out with the tender parts we are protecting. It is an invitation to meet the parts of ourselves that we have been defending against, sometimes at great length—things like anger or shame, which are often at the core of our blind spots—and to welcome them home.

Part of the reason these aspects of ourselves have stayed away from home is that we fear experiencing them, and that's because we don't know how to deal with them. Self-compassion is the magic elixir for that fear because it brings ease to our nervous system. It gives us a base from which to mindfully experience with less judging what was pushed down, and a place from which to practice stepping into our alive, authentic expression in the world.

Bless Your Heart

Self-compassion and clear insight into blind spots are strongly interwoven. This is because when we come to understand that the blind spot effect—the methods we've been using to go after acceptance and love that cause us pain and confusion—doesn't work, clear seeing using the lens of compassion becomes the only possibility that makes sense! It springs out of the heart naturally when we stop judging ourselves and connect with the reality of what we see and discover.

"Embracing the suck"—welcoming everything that arises when we discover a blind spot—must coexist with self-compassion. But we don't need to focus *only* on the suck part, on what feels off or wrong or needs attention—such as anxiety, an entrenched belief, a moment of conflict with a loved one, or pain in our body. We can allow all of that to be there *and* at the same time have a moment of softness and kindness for ourselves.

For a shortcut route to a moment of self-compassion, I like to say to myself, *Bless my heart,* and then follow that with a statement about the truth of my experience: *Bless my heart, I'm doing the best I know how* or *Bless my heart, I am out of my element and I don't feel like I fit in right now* or *Bless my heart, I don't have clarity in this situation.* It's happening anyway, so why not stop resisting it? Bless your heart and then name it instead! We often think we will lose our drive forward and become doormats to life if we stop resisting what we don't like. Not true—we'll lose our *reactivity* and become available to meet the moment with wisdom. Reactivity that stems from resistance to what is happening comes from blindness and isn't our most authentic response. *Responsiveness,* by contrast, is an alive, spontaneous action appropriate to the moment. Acts of self-compassion, like pausing to be kind toward an uncomfortable feeling and listening at a deeper level to what is happening, can make a huge difference in whether we react or respond.

PRACTICE "Bless My Heart"

Here's a practice that can help you calm your inner judgment.

- Sit comfortably, and think about an aspect of your life that could use a little kindness right now. It might be something you're dealing with as a result of uncovering a blind spot. It might even be the fact that you haven't yet broken through and seen any of the behaviors or strategies you've been using that no longer serve you. Or it could be something completely unrelated, like a situation you're facing that feels charged and difficult. (Doing this practice around things unrelated to blind spots will help you deal with those hidden things when they do surface.)

- Take a moment to give the situation or yourself a feeling of kindness. Share from your heart a phrase like *Bless my heart, I'm doing the best I know how.* Feel free to place your hand on your heart or give yourself a hug as you do this.

- Notice how just the act of being warm and open toward yourself and the situation can shift feelings of intensity or judgment.

- Allow it all to be here as it is—the situation, your feelings about it, the act of kindness toward yourself—without resisting. Notice what you feel.

- Now, allow a spontaneous response to come to you that would meet the situation with wisdom, clarity, and kindness. If you *respond* instead of reacting, what will you do? You may decide, coming from a responsive, wise place, to take no action at all. You may decide to speak to someone or tell yourself a difficult truth. Whatever comes to you, allow it to guide you as you navigate this situation.

- If you need to repeat your *Bless my heart* phrase a few times as you consider your response, waiting for that moment of warmth and openness to unfold, that is fine. The more you practice this, the more easily that moment will arrive.

Vulnerability: The Portal to Wholeness

If learning to illuminate blind spots helps us integrate our shadowed parts into the wholeness of who we are, and the practice of self-compassion helps us welcome them, vulnerability—dropping our defenses so we can freely experience what is present—is the portal through which those parts return. We can't see and welcome these aspects of ourselves that arise in any given moment, such as a harsh belief or challenging emotion or a hurt from the past, without being undefended and soft to whatever comes. Otherwise we're just doing more of the same unkind thing: refusing our experience from a place of judgment.

Vulnerability arises when self-kindness allows us to lower our defenses. It is the act of being honest with what is present, but also opening our heart in an unguarded way to look, meet, and welcome what is there. The traditional definition of vulnerability is "the quality of being exposed to the possibility of attack or harm." What we do when our blind spots are revealed to us is to acknowledge what is soft and tender and hurting, and open to it with a loving heart. We're exposing it, but from a place of strength and self-kindness that lets us glean wisdom from where we've been lost.

It takes incredible fortitude to open to what hurts, as well as to share that with another. No wonder we resist: it's hardwired in us to pull in and defend when we are exposed and vulnerable. The ultimate terror is to be rejected, to be kicked out of the tribe, to be refused and scoffed, to be blamed. We go to such great lengths to avoid these things we fear, like hiding our mistakes or the parts of us that we feel don't fit in with those around us. Yet the healing happens through drawing close and being seen just as we are, without hiding from or avoiding what that looks like—admitting a mistake or revealing a tender or wounded part of ourselves, and opening to what is closed.

I asked leadership coach and consultant Wendy Appel, who has spent considerable time studying blind spots and their hidden gifts, what her biggest blind spot was. Here's what she told me:

> I've bumped into so many blind spots over the years but
> the one that still plagues me (I am still blind to some of
> its manifestations) is showing vulnerability. I have this
> need to appear competent; like I've got it together and
> know what I'm talking about or to acknowledge help
> received. I'm afraid if I show certain kinds of vulnerability,
> it will somehow be used against me—people won't hire
> me, will take advantage of me, won't want to hang out
> with me. . . . The context doesn't seem to matter—work,
> friendship, love, family. Intellectually, I know that
> under the right circumstances, showing vulnerability is

absolutely the best path forward and will get me what I desire, but it is discerning when, where, and how.

Can you relate? I can!

It's All Relationship

You might have noticed that this book focuses on looking at your own blind spots and doing the work of bringing self-compassion to your own vulnerabilities, not on uncovering other people's blind spots. There's a reason for that. Yes, everyone around you has blind spots too, and they need compassion just like you do, and you need to learn how to navigate your relationships as you uncover your blind spots and see the blind spots of others. But if you jump too quickly to the interpersonal realm, you may miss out on building the skills you need to bring to the table in your relationships. You can't skip over the intrapersonal realm: your relationship with yourself.

It goes like this. If I deeply, truly am not refusing myself and I know how to welcome all of who I am, if I understand my resistance to life, and if I am in touch with the idiosyncratic ways in which I try to get my own needs met, that will translate directly into my relationships. It can't *not* do that. If my mom walks into the room appearing angry, and I have no space in myself for my own anger, do you think there is a chance in Hades that I will be able to meet my mom in that moment in a way that would be skillful and kind? If because of my blind spots I have become skilled at avoiding my own anger, I may say to her, "Mom, look on the bright side! Stop being so upset—it helps nobody!" Or if I tend to lack self-regulation and act out my anger without self-awareness, I may react in anger in return: "Geez, chill out! Stop being so freaking annoyed! You're pissing me off!" Can you see how the number-one relationship we are building is the relationship with ourselves? If you learn kindness to yourself because you know it's the wisest response and you've learned it meets your most essential needs, you will transpose that insight and knowledge to others naturally because it's already inside of you. In contrast, if you start by trying to focus on how you treat others, you may be doing it to get those core needs of safety, belonging, and acceptance met, and then you'll be on the hook to those around you for your happiness. That may work temporarily but it doesn't create lasting change and meaningful self-awareness that can be expressed spontaneously in any situation. Pausing to get in touch with what is alive in us and learning how to do that in a nonjudgmental way will stand us in good stead as we navigate our relational lives.

•

Now I invite you to apply the concepts outlined in this chapter—easing defensiveness, welcoming vulnerability, softening judgment, Natural Self-Compassion practice, and *Bless my heart*—in taking a first look at one of your blind spots.

PRACTICE   The Big Reveal

Do you have a sense by now of areas in which you might be blind? We've looked at how we are blind in our unconscious biases, in first impressions and love, in our emotional worlds, and in the core stories that form the way we perceive who we are in the world. Now it's time for the big reveal. Are you ready?

- Sit quietly, and let yourself get centered. Or go to a nearby coffee shop and settle in with a journal and a warm drink—wherever is a good setting for you to inquire.

- Make sure you have a pencil and plenty of paper nearby.

- Now fill in the blank in the following statement. Welcome whatever bubbles up and write it down. If there is more than one ending to the statement, write them all down. If something comes up that seems to make no sense, write it down anyway. If it really doesn't fit, you can discard it later. "As I reflect upon what I've read so far, my biggest blind spot is _____."

- Let yourself be surprised by what comes up, whether you don't think you have a blind spot or you're overwhelmingly certain about what yours is, or anything in between. Start writing, and keep writing for as long as feels comfortable for you. Let the innate wisdom you have come through.

- If you don't know where to start or nothing is coming to you, write about where you go blind with a core belief (see chapter 4, page 82) or recycled emotion (chapter 5, page 95), and allow yourself to access your natural wisdom as you note what stands in the way of your seeing clearly in these areas.

- After you finish, return to the Five Mindful Breaths (chapter 1, page 17) or Natural Self-Compassion practice (this chapter, page 130), and notice what you feel. This is far more a process and journey than a destination and final discovery. Simply participating in the act of reflection is enough for you to be included in the community that is working toward seeing where we are blind and being more fully ourselves.

- If it feels right, share with a friend or loved one how that process was for you (no need to share what you wrote, just how it was to do the act of reflection on blind spots).

Congratulations! That was brave! And hopefully you gained some insights about yourself. Now we're ready to enter the fascinating territory of what others think our blind spots are. This is one of the best ways to find out what we are missing that is right in front of us. So let's embrace the suck together—the beautiful mess, the full catastrophe—as we open our minds and hearts toward how other people perceive us.

8

F*CK FEEDBACK
Illuminating How Others See Us

You ask of my companions.
Hills, sir, and the sundown, and a dog large as myself . . .
They are better than beings because they know, but do not tell . . .
EMILY DICKINSON, Letters, April 26, 1862[1]

THIS CHAPTER WAS originally titled "See Yourself as Others See You." Then I asked my entire family, my close friends, and a thousand friends on Facebook to point out my blind spots to me. By the end of this exploration I realized that "F*ck Feedback" said it much better!

Let's face it: hearing someone say, "I have some feedback for you" makes you want to run away from the person saying it. It doesn't have a very compassionate ring to it, so it puts you on the defensive, and you know it can be code for "I'm angry or disappointed in you and I'm going to tell you what you did that didn't work for me." Who wants to invite that?

But to shine a light on our own blind spots we *truly need* the people we trust most—therapists, friends, partners, and candid acquaintances—to help us see what we can't see ourselves. Our blind spots may *show up* in behaviors, but as we've seen, they *originate* in places that are hidden or shadowed, and they contain feelings such as shame, guilt, or a vulnerability that we haven't acknowledged and allowed. When we explore them with someone who knows us and *wants the best for us* (very important), finding these hidden places helps us tap the gifts they hold. This may get a little uncomfortable at times, but believe me, it's worth it.

Ask for Supportive Reflection—Not Feedback

If you engage in this exercise, and I hope you do, be sure to proceed with caution. Illuminating blind spots with the support of the insights of others is not the same as getting feedback in the way the term is often used—like a performance review or a report card. In my own exploration I discovered that when people think you're asking for *feedback* on your blind spots instead of what you really need—thoughtful, contemplative support—it can get in the way of genuine discovery.

I'll wager that no one has ever asked you, or anyone you know, for that matter, to help them find their blind spots. That means we haven't had any practice in doing it. So there will be a tendency to look for what's *wrong* instead of what's *hidden*, and frankly, that can get messy. The deal is that if we simply ask friends and family to name our blind spots, they will probably revert to the feedback model of telling us what they like or don't like —because *that*, they know how to do. Or they will speak from a narrow perception that doesn't capture a real pattern, saying, for example, "You are critical" instead of "I see a pattern that when you feel anxious you tend to criticize those around you, and I wonder what may lie beneath that." See the difference? Partly this is because everyone will have their own idea about what a blind spot is, and lots of people will think it's about *behavior*. Consider comments like these:

> "You ignore me when I'm trying to tell you something,
> and you should listen better."

> "You don't seem to know what you want in life and you
> need to take the bull by the horns and figure it out."

> "You are too rushed and you don't seem to have time for
> me—I need you to be more punctual and less distracted
> so we can connect."

Part of the reason they offer observations like this is that they are seeing you through their own filter—even through their own blind spots!—and that can get tricky. And if they view this as their golden chance to tell you the things they've been stewing about, it's not likely to be much help and it actually may inflict a lot of hurt. So what you really need to do is to clearly emphasize that you are looking for the hidden things *that drive you*, not the ways you behave when you're acting from that drive. Again, see the difference? What you're after is the stuff you may be out of touch with (blind to) but that will be transformative when revealed. They may *describe* behaviors as they share their reflections but are doing so within the context of your growth and healing, not judgment. It's a tall order!

Blind spot reflection (not feedback) sounds like this:

> You have an underlying need for safety and acceptance, as we all do, but it can motivate you to push down what you know to be true and instead accommodate others. When you go blind to this, you get into messes and your life starts to reflect that—like that time when you kept that troublesome employee on staff when you really wanted to let him go. Because you were too afraid to hurt him and to deal with the impact of his leaving, you caused your team at work tremendous stress and undue suffering. Everyone else bore the brunt of your actions, which accommodated him at your and your team's expense.
>
> Your truth may seem scary because speaking it will have an impact on others, but my sense is that you can trust that doing your best at sharing it will help up-level your life. I'm wondering if you can see a way you could have handled that situation if you had spoken from your truth and seen this underlying dynamic at play. Could you still have met those needs for safety and acceptance, but in a different way?

Of course, most people, being unaccustomed to doing this, might not be so refined or articulate in their support as they peer into your psyche, but you can still compile the behaviors people point out and do the investigative work on your own to reveal the underlying dynamics.

To look at the distinction between feedback and reflection another way:

> Feedback is motivated by someone wanting you to change the way you are.

> Reflection is motivated by someone wanting you to grow.

One has an agenda and the other doesn't. The first comes from aggression at some level: *Please change so that I can feel better, or so you can be a better version of yourself* for me.

The second comes from love and compassion: *I want you to see more clearly and suffer less (and create less suffering).*

You can see that the kind of reflection you're looking for requires a certain degree of insight and wisdom from the person you're asking. And the bummer is that very few us are friends with the Dalai Lama. So how do we even broach the subject, and how do we best connect with our support networks to help us discover what is hidden?

Asking for Reflection

As I said up front, I became my own blind spot guinea pig. I reached out to my network (I really couldn't write a book on blind spots without doing so, could I?) and it turned out to be a surprisingly emotional time; at one point I found myself on my living room floor crying. It had been years since I had felt that level of emotion. My reaction wasn't in response to the information I received—that part was okay, although not always easy. It was from some tough conversations that ensued, as it brought up family dynamics that had comfortably been relegated to the shadows. So be prepared: when you ask for a blind spot to be revealed, you can't know what you'll get—that's the nature of blind spots. For me there was a happy conclusion; my family is good at working stuff out, so we grew and learned from the process. That's what I want for you too!

I think that part of what we fear about loved ones surfacing a blind spot is that it will define us. *Oh, no, I can't handle disconnection!*

I'm overly sensitive! I'm a heartbreaker! But to embrace *all* of ourselves, we must face the dread of being defined by *one* part of ourselves. If you see whatever you discover as *a part of yourself returning home*, you won't have to defend against the truth of it. This is what I learned firsthand. And remember: the portal through which that part returns is your vulnerability, your undefended, open heart.

Guidelines for the Ask

I learned some things about how to approach asking for this form of support by experimenting with this. Here are some resulting tips.

- Ask someone you trust and who has been consistently reliable in their advice and assessment. Make sure it's someone you feel sees and understands you, and doesn't judge you.

- Ask someone with whom you are in regular touch. Avoid asking friends and family you see, say, twice a year unless there is a special reason why you'd like to ask them.

- Make this whole idea simple and nonthreatening for them. If you're soliciting support through email, give clear direction and requests. If it's going to be an in-person conversation, prepare them in the same way ahead of time.

- Be vulnerable. Let them know this isn't easy for you, but it's important because you want to learn and grow.

- Ask for support. Appeal to their generosity toward you. Tell them that illuminating what is hidden to you will be a great gift to you.

- Be open to learning. Even if what you receive isn't what you would have hoped to hear, let yourself find the truth that resonates with you. You can then discard the rest.

HOW TO SAY IT

Here are a few examples of how you might word the ask.

- "I am looking at my blind spots—stuff I don't see about myself that may *drive* me unconsciously (remember, you're getting at drives, not behaviors) or that may be hidden to me—and I need help in seeing what I might be missing. I understand that my blind spot may hold a shadow part of myself that I've pushed down and don't want to acknowledge. It would be such a gift to get to see and experience it, to bring it into the light. Perhaps it is some unrecognized form of my own power or aliveness. Can you help me find that gift?"

- "Do you see that I have any blind spots—something that may be obvious to you but that you can tell I don't see about myself, something that may drive my behavior and cause me to miss a hidden gift that can help me grow?"

- You can also leave blind spots out of the equation: "Can you tell me about any hidden gifts you see in me that may help me grow? Something I may not be consciously in touch with that, were I to discover it, might stop me from doing unconscious behaviors and get me more in touch with my power?"

- You can also just flat out say, "Do I have blind spots that are obvious to you?"

Any version of the above, or your own articulation, will be fine. Just be sure to point out that you are looking for insight, not for what is wrong! Remember to define what a blind spot is, in your own words (or borrowing some of my words from the preceding list). Put it into language you feel comfortable with and that will resonate with your friends and family. Get ready to be a little misunderstood, as that is part of the process too! But if you ask the right people, you should get gems of insight. Even if you ask the wrong people, you might still find some gems.

Okay, I Got the Info: Now What?

Once you've had some conversations and unearthed the nuggets in these reflections on your blind spots, what's next? There are probably a number of ways you can take the next step, but let me share what I did. Once I had received my blind spot reflections from a number of people, I did four things:

- I threw everything into one document.

- I printed it out and took some time to mindfully read every word, highlighting what stood out to me as important.

- I looked for patterns; I think this is key in sorting through the "noise" to get to the heart of things. I found that different people said similar things about my need for safety or about a particular behavior they noticed.

- When I was ready to explore further, I had conversations with some of the people who responded to clarify what they had offered and make sure I had gleaned all of their insights.

The ideal scenario is to allow this process to take a few weeks, time enough to ask for reflections, sort through them, let them sink in, and then circle back and have conversations with the generous souls who shared them with you. When the unconscious becomes conscious—when the shadow comes into light—you will need time to understand and make sense of what is now in plain view. I took walks and talked on the phone with my partners in this exercise, reflecting, allowing time for unfolding conversations to happen.

Remember as you go along to be aware of and let go of any critical or judgmental voices—toward yourself or others. There's no point in judging yourself for the reflections you received, or in judging others for giving it! Always keep the purpose of this effort in sight: to learn and grow. It's so easy to come at this with a desire to change ourselves so we can be more liked and accepted. Yet if we do that, we miss the chance to welcome home the part of ourselves that has been knocking at our door and asking for attention and care.

As you surface and meet what is blind to you, watch for any feelings of shame or insufficiency, as those feelings are natural too. Welcome them and get to know them as friends, letting them come and go. Let yourself speak the truth too; if the reflection hurt you, you can say that. It's all part of the process. Remember that your motivation is to be more fully yourself, more integrated, less blind. It's not to be more perfect, more ideal, or less messy—you are not doing this to "fix" yourself or meet someone else's ideal of you. That is the key distinction that will help you grow.

Working with the Reflections You Receive

To give you a better sense of how to work with the insights you receive, let's have a look at some concrete things that you could potentially hear. Then I'll offer ways you might process that information.

1 "When others hurt you, you ignore it or go into denial about it, and you stay too long in situations that are causing you emotional suffering because of your desire to be nice and to see the best in people. I wonder if you have an underlying need for security that causes this."

2 "Your need to be right makes you not truly listen to others. You are so insistent on proving your point and being the expert that you can't hear another point of view. You come across as arrogant and superior and I'm wondering what is underneath that. What is at stake for you?"

3 "When you hurt others, in order to stay blameless and safe from attack, you blame the one you hurt. That means you tend not to learn from conflict, and that causes the conflict to cycle again and again."

4 "You hide your power when you're around men in the workplace. It's as if you turn off your true self in order to be invisible, and you lose your voice and autonomy. And it only happens around men. I wonder what that's about, what ideas you hold that may cause this behavior."

5 "You're always trying to get other people to notice you and give you attention, and it never seems like it's enough. It's hard to be around you sometimes because it's like you have to be the center of attention and everyone else exists to make you feel worthy or loved. What part of yourself are you ignoring that might make you behave like this?"

It is helpful to get this kind of honest reflection, because it helps us see the patterns that weren't obvious. It also helps us clarify where those views feel right-on, or a little off base. Sometimes people misperceive us, as we misperceive others—that is part of being human. For me, it has been key to understand this and to search for the truth—*my own truth*—in any given situation while also being open to hearing others' points of view. Other people's perceptions don't have to threaten or define me. Remember our tendency to believe we are right? Some of the people you ask to reflect on your blind spots might be in the ballpark but batting zero, some might be out in left field, and the most random person could hit a home run in their perceptions of you. Stay open! Even if something you hear may not feel 100 percent correct, that is part of the deal. Listening for the truth can help you understand how others view you and, hopefully, how they can support you in seeing yourself more clearly.

It's also good to separate out *intention* from *impact*. When we respond to the information we receive by trying to prove that our *intentions* are good, we can lose sight of the effects our blind spots have on others. Let in the possibility that others are seeing something about your impact that you may be completely blind to—and seeing it may be a huge gift! We can easily impact others without intending to, and it's part of our growth to get this and not be scared of it. Being open to what you *don't* know and *don't* see is a beautiful human quality worth reaching for.

Now let's look at some insights and gifts we might glean from the statements in the numbered list above, in order by number.

1 I need to connect with *myself* in order to be safe. This is a reminder to stay in my inner knowing (what is true and aligned for me) to gain that basic sense of safety and trust, rather than checking outside myself for safety by attuning to someone else, being too much in someone else's world. I need to acknowledge and allow in the hurt and pain others cause me through their actions. When I go into denial and act like everything is fine, I don't help myself. I can take that as a sign I may be avoiding a truth that I know deep down. My security can come from telling myself the truth rather than pushing it down and ignoring it. *The gift: Listen to my inner knowing. I can trust it; I have a strong sense of the truth.*

2 It's okay to not be right sometimes. When I was a kid, my parents used to tell me I didn't know anything, so I use being right as a type of defense against being close to others. I don't know how to connect from the heart, so I just speak from my head to try to stay safe. Softening around this need to be an expert and let others know me in the moment feels scary, but I think it's worth it. I want connection deep down and am willing to take the risk of dropping my strong opinions and opening my heart. *The gift: Stay in my heart because I can powerfully connect with generosity from there.*

3 I go on the attack when I feel someone is blaming me. Even if they are just expressing an emotion, I still take it as blame and I push them away. I think I blame myself deep down, so even when someone isn't blaming me I take it that way. My work is to let go of self-blame, and that will translate into a more

loving way to communicate during conflict and learn from it. It's frightening to see this pattern because I want to be perfect. I guess I need to allow the mess in a little bit in order to show up as the whole "me." *The gift: Acknowledge my innocence. It helps me communicate from a place of responsibility and love.*

4 I fall asleep to my voice and opinion at work and I don't even realize it. I just assume anything a man says is right, and I shouldn't speak up or contradict it. I turn into an eight-year-old girl who just follows along. I haven't seen this before, but now my commitment to myself is to be visible to myself first and foremost, to notice that I do this and catch myself in the moment, seeing my own power and autonomy. Once I do that, I'm committed to speaking and interacting from this self-visibility. *The gift: I'm incredibly powerful and independent. Seeing myself helps others see me.*

5 I love being the center of attention—I'm a natural ham. But sometimes it's too much for others. I feel desperate for attention, but I actually totally ignore myself when I act like this. If I give myself attention and care, I wonder if I will crave getting it from others less strongly. I'm willing to experiment with finding ways to care for myself because I don't want to be a drain on others, and I want to be a true friend. *The gift: I have a strong, magical presence and I want to nurture it by seeing myself clearly and taking care of myself.*

Processing What We Realize

It's important to take time to mindfully process the reflections you received, in whatever way feels right to you, even if you only reached out to one person. I'd suggest welcoming your experience as it is; let it be a starting point. Notice the emotions that arise—the beliefs, the shame, the joy—and compassionately listen for any strong messages that emerge. Some further examples are:

- This pattern of pushing people away keeps me from true intimacy and acceptance.

- The way I lose myself in certain scenarios is a pattern that happens only when I'm stressed or faced with someone like my mother.

- I tend to be powered by insecurity, and that forces me to be perfectionistic and to impose my views on others.

As you're processing, you may feel sadness and grief, or disconnection, or joy and connection, or you may cycle through a range of emotions. Let it all sink in, without judgment, and allow the patterns to light up like constellations in the night sky. Allow them to shine. There is indeed a message hidden in these stars if we gaze at them with no agenda. It takes courage to simply feel their impact, not judge too soon, not think we know too soon, and allow the mysterious work of the emergence of our vulnerable, tender heart.

"But . . . Ouch, This Must Be Off Base!"

After you have allowed yourself time with a piece of information you have received and find that it hurts and feels off base:

- Feel the hurt and be kind to yourself: *Bless my heart.*

- Say aloud what is true for you: "That hurt" or "That didn't land well and doesn't feel resonant." (That's self-compassion in action!)

- Let it be there without needing to mend the hurt or the brokenness in the relationship. Look truthfully at how you feel and its impact.

Examine the Patterns

What do you do when you see a pattern in the reflections?

- Step back and take a wide-lens view of the whole situation.

- Discard what is unimportant. (Remember how valuable it is to reduce the "noise" in the system?)

- Don't look for the obvious in what people say; look beneath it. Let yourself see what is right in front of you about this pattern, as if you're gazing at a painting that slowly reveals its beauty to you.

Asking for reflections from those around you is more about the process and journey than the specific insight you reach. The earlier chapters in this book about leaning into the unknown apply to these steps in real time: being curious and attentive in a fully alive exploration of how others see you helps you understand how you move through the world and where you defend yourself. The act of being curious and open speaks—and teaches—volumes. Seeing our blind spot helps us to see ourselves with more balance and lighthearted sobriety, and to see our own inner horizon, at the edge of which lie our greatest treasures.

●

When it comes to getting the most out of the observations and insights of others, walking is your friend. Get up and go for a walk, a meandering one with no agenda—an amble. Be open to insights that may come to you. Maybe you have been resisting this introspection—which is natural enough—or are only reflecting on the possibility of doing it. Spur yourself to action. Let yourself, or a tree, or the blue sky be your reflective and supportive mirror. Ask: *What insights can I gain from the information I have received?*

●

When you are able to identify your blind spots and receive their hidden gifts, you unleash a potent force that helps you navigate your life with greater clarity and wisdom: intuition. And happily enough, intuition makes it easier to uncover more of your blind spots! We'll discuss this in depth in chapter 9.

TRUST YOUR GUT

Uncovering Your Intuitional Navigation System

Good intuitions must go beyond the information given, and therefore, beyond logic.

GERD GIGERENZER[1]

A FRIEND OF MINE, the founder and president of a well-known leadership consultancy startup in San Francisco with a promising "runway" for success, recently faced a pivotal life decision. Just as his company was getting off the ground, landing big contracts, and wading waist deep into highly creative and well-funded projects, he was offered another job as CEO of a competing company. The offer forced him to choose between the company he had poured his heart and soul into and heading up another, more established organization with a team twice the size.

From the outside it looked like a clear choice: to stay with his own creation and see it through to the next stage. This would enable him to launch his own voice and work into the world and write the book he'd been longing to create, among other things. He had a great staff working for him and the vision was his—they needed him. His company was the new sexy consultancy on the block and its story was just starting to be written. Still, the offer pulled at him, and he found himself considering it.

One day while I was walking at the lake in my neighborhood, he called me and relayed his dilemma to me, saying with a mixture of curiosity and lighthearted angst, "Kelly, I don't know what to do. I was offered this position and even though I have so many reasons not to take it, I feel an intuitive pull toward it. I want to explore it if you have a few minutes to do so." He continued, listing out all the pros and cons of taking the offer and turning it down.

Gut intuition is a mysterious thing. It has its own life and its own currents, even when it flies in the face of our most rational ideas. As he spoke, I could hear that there was a sense of alignment or "yes" when he spoke about leaving his company to take the new job. Even though it fundamentally contradicted his ideas about who he was and what he should do, the clarity behind all of his questions and analytic processing was shining through: it felt *right* to him to take it. My job as a sounding board was simply to point that out and support his continued inquiry.

He took some long walks alone in nature, quietly reflecting, and consulted with other trusted friends and colleagues. He eventually made his decision: he left his own brainchild for the CEO position, and has since said it was without a doubt the best choice he could have made, with positive ripple effects in many directions. The act took courage, because he had to be willing to let others down and possibly be perceived in a negative light. And it was a personal risk; he had a family to consider and was in a hard-earned position of security that was largely under his own control. Yet even with those elements factored in, his commitment to his own personal integrity and to listening to his intuition kept the perceived risk from getting in the way of acting on his inner knowing.

Shortly before taking the job, he described to me that he just had a felt sense that it was "right," and while he could give logical reasons for the move, the primary motivator was his gut feeling. When he realized he was leaning that way, he had checked it out with friends, asking if he had a blind spot they could see or if he was missing anything. At some point it became a "choiceless choice": the answer revealed itself, and he had to follow it.

When something feels "right," it doesn't mean the situation is bull's-eye perfect and will provide unending happiness and bliss. Rather, it means the situation is aligned and we are on track with taking the next step in the unfolding (choose your own adventure) story of our lives. When we act in alignment with our inner knowing and intuitive sense, there is a feeling of "rightness" that carries signature qualities: alignment, ease, flow, and a natural "yes." A lack of resistance. It's a form of knowing that doesn't assert itself, yet is clear as day. I call this the *100 percent "yes."* And I have discovered for myself, in my work and relationships, that anything less than a 100 percent "yes" is a "no." This doesn't mean that I don't make decisions that involve sacrifice or compromise—I do. Or that I never change course after making one of those decisions; I do that too. But when I say yes to something that has, say, a 75 percent feeling of "yes," I usually get exactly what I signed up for: it turns out there's a 25 percent "no" in the mix.

Waking Up to Intuition

Because it frees you to see more clearly, illuminating your blind spots helps you access this natural intuition and life wisdom and keeps you from getting bogged down in other fixed ways of seeing. And as a result, you make better decisions: Who doesn't want that? Your intellect and reason are still involved, but you aren't a slave to your ideas any longer. And let's face it: How can you objectively know how things should go anyway? The thing about trusting your intuition and acting from it is that the next moment always comes, carrying with it a new opportunity to listen and respond spontaneously to each new possibility. And when this becomes a habit, even when you are faced with the biggest challenges of your life, you can still navigate from a place of openness, curiosity, and listening for the next best step. When your blind spots drop away, you can welcome feelings of loss, heartache, and fear of change and step into the next wild, unknown moment—feeling your way in.

Let's say that instead of being tuned in to his inner wisdom, my friend had been operating from a blind spot of inadequacy: despite his outward success, thinking he was not worthy enough to take further risks ("my success was a fluke") and believing he was better off playing it safe. Do you think he would have taken the leap? Probably not. You can think of it as a kind of formula. If your vision is 50 percent clear yet 50 percent stuck in the shadows of your fixed ideas about others and the world around you, or your own self-limiting beliefs, chances are your decisions are going to be about half on the mark. That's a pretty good incentive to illuminate your blind spots! When we see through our blind spots and work with them, we enable ourselves to face the truth and no longer have to defend against it.

The Power of the Felt Sense

We waste precious energetic resources when we defend against what is right in front of us and see what's not really there. In contrast, seeing clearly allows us to gain access to our body's natural wisdom in the form of signals that come through the felt sense of the body. These signals are often outside of our conscious awareness or rational processes, and require space, time, and reflection to be heard (they are like the still, small voice that whispers instead of whacking us on the head). If we are checked out from our bodies and the messages they transmit in the form of sensations and emotions, we block access to what is right in front of us: valuable information that supports us in finding our true north. But as we mindfully meet, greet, and welcome *all* of who we are, we are better able to clear the noise (the false beliefs, unconscious biases, and suppressed emotions) in the signal and listen to what is clear, simple, and most true for us in any given moment. Our defenses against the world are softened, and that makes all the difference in the world.

What Is a Gut Feeling?

So what exactly is intuition anyway? Check this guy out: there's been a boatload of research on intuition, its fallibility, and its trustworthiness, and Gerd Gigerenzer is a star player in the field.

Gigerenzer is a German social psychologist, director of the Max Planck Institute for Human Development in Berlin, and an advocate for the efficacy and power of human intuition and gut instincts. If Daniel Kahneman popularized and articulated the notion of human *fallibility* by illuminating blind spots in decision-making and intuition (the mental shortcuts we discussed earlier), Gigerenzer popularized and articulated that of human *trustability*. They both talk about reasoning, risk calculation, decision-making, and intuition, yet Kahneman articulates when rules of thumb and intuition *don't* work and Gigerenzer articulates when they *do*. The way I see it, they are saying the same thing but coming at it from different directions, balancing each other out.

The experiments Kahneman and Tversky performed on mental shortcuts aren't based on the unpredictability of everyday human life, says Gigerenzer, but rather on mathematical risk calculation and logic problems, and as such, they have inaccurately fostered an idea in the public sphere that human intuition and our associated decisions are faulty.[2] We do go wrong, yet he asserts that there's something we can all agree on as humans: *that we tend to trust our instincts*. Gigerenzer is interested in illuminating the ways we go right so we can learn to make better decisions. Our intuitions hold such a powerful and convincing pull. Yes, they can pull us in the wrong direction, but that's not the full story. So why is that? When do unconscious mental shortcuts, or rules of thumb, work for us? How can we harness the power of our intuition to make better decisions?

The Freedom to Not "Know"

Life is complex, and, without thinking much about it, we make the assumption that our answers to life's most pressing challenges and questions should be equally complex. We think we need to take into account all factors and carefully measure out our best response. Sometimes, though, a gut intuition without an explanation can be freeing—and *we need permission to not always know the reasons we do what we do*.

Gigerenzer argues that reasoning can be at odds with intuition, and it's not always helpful to know why or how you did something. And he discovered something interesting: when people are asked to give reasons for their choices (such as why they chose to buy one kind of jam over another), *they are less satisfied with their choice than when they don't give a reason*.[3] It turns out that people are more satisfied when they have a limited search and then settle on one option as opposed to continuing to search for an alternative, or weighing pros and cons and describing how they reached their decision. It's actually stressful to have to explain all of our choices, especially those based upon our felt intuition. We can't always find the right reason for what we do—one explanation for why arguments can be tiring and unfruitful. It's easy on the mind to stay simple (I'd like raspberry jam, please!), and it works (Because I feel like it!)

In a *Harvard Business Review* interview, Gigerenzer shared that about 50 percent of all decision processes that are engaged in by the leadership of large international companies end with a gut decision. That's a huge number! And then, of course, because making decisions this way is not generally accepted, the leadership team hires consultants to explain in hindsight why their decision was right-on! They seek out "proof." But as with the choice of jam, it's not satisfying to backfill like that, and it's not necessarily helpful. It creates a story about the past and its apparent certainty that may not be quite accurate.[4] Says Gigerenzer, "In hindsight there is no uncertainty left. . . . In foresight, however, we must face uncertainty."[5]

I would add to this: in *present-sight*, when our seeing is clear and our intuition is activated, we are open to what is without clinging to certainty or trying to eliminate or predict what is uncertain. And in that place of flow, we are comfortable with ambiguity and confident in our capacity to act on what we know from moment to moment. And we are less likely to make decisions based in blind spots than from being in touch with our intuitive truth.

Recognizing a Gut Feeling

Gigerenzer has identified three components of intuitions, or gut feelings, the presence of that still, small voice:

1 They appear quickly in consciousness.

2 We aren't fully cognizant of the underlying reasons behind their appearance.

3 They are strong enough to act upon.[6]

When you think about it, this makes sense. The mental shortcuts and cognitive biases that Kahneman brought to light are real, but they aren't the only drivers of our decision-making, and sometimes they are the *right* drivers, as he freely admits. There are times when it is right to trust your gut feeling: when it isn't operating from *inaccurate biases* but rather, using the *right rule* in the *right instance*.

For example, if you have little information and the environment in which you are making a decision is complex and uncertain, that's a good time to trust your intuition or gut instinct. Both Daniel and Gerd agree on that one. With so many variables and unknowns, it's better to just trust your hunch than to make a list and check it twice. Of course, you can feel free to make a list. But the types of decisions that occur in moments of uncertainty, unpredictability, and complexity call for simple, gut-based solutions that *incorporate* contextual information but aren't *bound to* rules of logic and reason. When you have a lot of predictability and a lot of information, on the other hand, you can feel free to make lists and rely heavily on your analytical mind.

Intuitive Choice Rules of Thumb

What are some concrete examples of when we should trust our gut? According to Gigerenzer, in moments of uncertainty, complexity, and few known variables, you're likely to be guided by a few rules of thumb that are right-on:

- Less-is-more

- Recognition

- Take-the-best

The less-is-more rule of thumb refers to the fact that if you have too much knowledge, you can't rely on your intuition. For example, Germans guessed the answer to this question more correctly than did Americans: Which city is bigger, Detroit or Milwaukee? This is the less-is-more rule in action; they didn't have a lot of knowledge about

American cities, and they'd never heard of Milwaukee, but they had heard of Detroit so assumed it was bigger.

The recognition rule of thumb applies here as well—they recognized "Detroit," so they figured that was the answer. And both this rule and the less-is-more rule were at work in an experiment about stock market trading as well; total novices who knew nothing about the stock market outperformed expert stock traders in guessing which stocks would rise! It was because they had less information, and they only chose the names of companies they recognized when they did the exercise.[7]

The recognition rule of thumb is also called "go with what you know," according to Gigerenzer. If people had never heard of *any* companies in the stock market, they would perform poorly, of course—at chance levels. But guess what: if you know all the companies, you also operate at chance levels—like the so-called experts! It's good to know *something*, but not knowing a lot can help you make a correct intuitive guess. The experts are so blinded by their information that their guesses are rendered useless. In other words, they are blinded by what they see—they know too much.

The take-the-best rule of thumb is a one-reason argument. You have a hunch based on one reason, and you go for it, focusing on that reason and ignoring the rest. That too is likely to turn out well. Take the exotic bird of paradise and its colorful mating dance, an example Gigerenzer uses. I get that birds of paradise aren't humans, but they do it too. They are the wildest-looking creatures, with brilliant plumes and they do crazy-ass footwork. The males set up their dance floor like a bunch of OCD hippies, moving branches and clearing the floor of twigs and leaves, and then cut loose. But after all this kerfuffle, the females simply choose the birds with the longest tail! What is important for the female bird of paradise is to ignore the "right" information (how clean the male's dirty dancing floor is and how wild his plumage looks—that's for competition with the other males) and focus on the *actual* right information (I need the longest tail so I can birth a baby birdie that also has a long tail and will keep our genes in the gene pool).[8]

Meanwhile, back to humans. Our intuitive system, argues Gigerenzer, has developed a *capability* to use these rules of thumb, and our life experience and learning help us develop the *capacity* to know when to use which one. Practicing intuitive decision-making—being willing to experiment and make choices based on gut feelings—helps us build that capacity. We learn which "right" information to ignore, and which right information to focus on. Remember Alice in the meeting (chapter 4)? She turned the capability we have as human beings to not personalize other people's drama into a capacity. She ignored the "right" information and, with insight, saw the real right information. This kind of learning is all beneath our conscious awareness. We learn when our gut leads us astray—like when we fall in love on account of the halo effect—and when our gut leads us in a beneficial direction, like when we fall in love with our eyes open. Going off track actually helps us get back on track, and getting on track helps us understand the markers and signposts that accompany being in this kind of alignment.

All told, what's important is to learn from experience. When we are blinded by our filters we have a hard time learning, because we are spending time with the wrong information at the wrong time. Mindful awareness of what is relevant and present right in front of us helps us learn better and stop missing what is obvious, like happy little algorithms!

As we touched on earlier in the book, an algorithm is a learning function or a way to process data (typically using a computer) that operates by a few rules and that can learn from its complex environment. It doesn't need to know everything about the environment to make relatively accurate decisions; too much of the wrong input will only confuse it. Leslie Valiant, a computer scientist, shares that "an algorithm can operate within an environment about which it does not have initial knowledge and that is also more complex than itself, and yet can successfully perform 'approximately correct' learnings if it can interact extensively with the environment and learn from it."[9] This can help us relax: we get that life is unpredictable and complex so we allow ourselves to be simple in the face of that. We take each moment as a new one, bringing along with us what we have learned, of course, but releasing the hold of our self-control that comes from the illusion that we are in control. Not making an effort where we don't need to make one, and not taking it all so seriously. That is a serious life hack right there.

Major Blind Spot: The Illusion of Control

One of the secrets of accessing our inner knowing is to let go of a *big* collective blind spot we share: the illusion of control. When we can do that, we can spend more time in a state of flow, taking life as it actually comes, in *present-sight*, rather than living under the mistaken impression that we can (or should be able to) control everything that comes our way.

We like to think we are in control but if we look at the facts, it's very clear that we're not. A meteor could be hurtling toward the Earth right now. Every second that passes, we don't really *know* if we will still be alive for the next one. Of course, there are a lot of things we do control, like planning the launch of an app or taking out the trash or booking a flight or preparing to have a baby, but at the most basic and existential level we just plain old aren't in control. Similarly to the hindsight bias, we think the future is knowable because the past seems to be knowable, but when it's unpacked, even the past isn't as knowable as we assume. It is our coherent stories and blind spots that help us believe we are in control—an illusion—in order to help us maintain homeostasis, feel good, and bebop our way through our lives. No problem; it's innocent, and it works—except when it limits us by keeping us from living a freer, more creative life, or when it keeps us defended against the inevitable ups and downs we all face. When we are in a state of refusal that comes from a need to be in control, we suffer.

What if, by acknowledging uncertainty and ambiguity and opening ourselves to the truth of it, we can free ourselves to be in a flow state, deeply in touch with our intuition and inner knowing? What if—even though we think it's the scariest thing to let go of control—it's the *wisest* thing to do? We assume that we are rational and can figure everything out. But what if we factored in our own ignorance—along with a healthy dose of complexity, such as the astounding fact that we are these bipedal creatures roaming around on Earth riding elevators, flying in airplanes, ordering cappuccinos, growing tomatoes, procreating, and living in communities—and started relying more on the felt sense of what we know to be the best action in any given moment? We would be released from much anxiety. We wouldn't feel like we had to do things exactly right—and get depressed when we didn't—or put pressure on ourselves to have the bull's-eye answer before taking action. If we could only relax into letting go, our decisions and actions could feel more congruent and easeful because they wouldn't carry with them the weight of the world.

When we are no longer blind, our view of the world comes from present-sight: the noise in the signal is reduced, and we can navigate intuitively more of the time, operating from a deep connection with ourselves and the world around us. This is emotional intelligence in action.

Depending on how much noise is in our signal today, it may take a while to learn from this new way of navigating life, and we need to give ourselves room to make "mistakes" and take risks. But we truly can give ourselves the freedom to get in touch with what is most deeply alive and to listen to it, and learn from it.

Returning to Home Base

The more you use your newly accessible intuition, the more practice you will get in making truth-based decisions, and the more clearly you will see your previously unconscious judgments and patterns. It is a process of continually removing "static" from the system. You are putting yourself into a *self-reinforcing loop of deeper levels of discovery* (of yourself, and of reality as it is without your unconscious filters). You have ever greater access to wise action and discriminative wisdom, just like a happy little algorithm. And that gets you ever closer to "home base."

Home base is where your intuition functions most naturally. It is your authentic, natural self expressing in the world: imperfect yet real, restful yet alive, in touch with your inner guidance system of knowing and truth. It's so helpful, in your work with blind spots, to get to know what it feels like to leave your home and what it's like to come back home.

Have you ever heard sin defined as "missing the mark"? Home is resting on the mark, a quality of flow and presence to your life, awake to what you are experiencing. It's deeply settling to find yourself at home. It's not perfect, and it's not something you can describe to other people, but there's an ease in your natural knowing.

We learn by understanding our own home base and experimenting with what it feels like to be near to or far from it (think Big Bird on *Sesame Street* running up to the camera saying, "Neeeearr" and running away from the camera as he says, "Faaaarrr"). Trusting your gut is learning what "near" and "far" mean for you in regard to alignment with your inner knowing, and since we learn like little algorithms, why not do it mindfully?

One way I have learned to discover home for myself is through a years-long mentorship with John Prendergast, spiritual teacher, psychotherapist, and author of *In Touch: How to Tune In to the Inner Guidance of Your Body and Trust Yourself*. When John and I sit together, we attune to each other and to the moment. We may do silent gazing, resting in a shared, spacious presence, but it feels timeless because it is experienced without an agenda to get somewhere, figure something out, or be somebody. When we first began sitting together years ago, I was uncomfortable with the silence because I was faced with my own self-hatred and judgment, and saw so easily all the masks I wore in the presence of others. Over the years that melted away, and what is left as we sit together now is a shared attuned resonance that is beyond words: a return to home. This experience has helped me see that our intuition, our inner knowing, and our attunement to the softer, quieter things of life form the fertile ground from which to feel the truth of things and make wise decisions in life.

When we rest as we are in a quality of ease and well-being and allow actions to come from that place instead of our "rational" minds, we sense that we aren't separate from what is happening or from others. We use our minds but they are in service to our hearts and to this rested, open, deeply attuned and connected way of being. Our nervous systems get on board with this knowing when we can share in such an attuned and spacious way with another, and that gets transposed to all areas of life. And it's so helpful to find home base in yourself when you're in the presence of another person who is resting in their own home base, someone who welcomes all of who they are—including their own refusals, idiosyncrasies, and foibles. It helps you find that in yourself, because when they aren't refusing themselves, and they aren't refusing you either, it helps *you* stop refusing you too!

This is not a typical form of knowledge sharing because there are no directions, there is no manual, and there is nothing to learn except how to be yourself in another person's presence. I invite you to try it for yourself.

PRACTICE Finding Home Base with Another

Simply sitting in silence with another person for two minutes, gazing together, can change your life because it cuts through all your normal social interactions and gets to the heart of the shared experience of being human—the ultimate home base.

- Find a quiet and comfortable place for the two of you to sit, facing one another.

- You can share a soft focus on the floor between you, or you can look (not stare) directly into each other's eyes with a soft gaze. Simply be yourselves, together.

- There is no need to merge with the other person or do anything at all; just rest in your own presence while you share the silence with them.

- After two minutes, share with each other: "How was that?" and listen (and speak) without an agenda and with curiosity.

Now let's go solo in seeking out home base.

PRACTICE: Finding Home Base

To find home base on your own, you can ask two basic questions, and then follow up with clarifying questions to get to the essence of each. Think of a decision you are currently facing. Then ask yourself:

1 *How am I going away from home?* Where am I in resistance to being me, or in resistance to life, denying my experience to please another or trying to be a certain way? Where am I not telling myself the truth that I know?

2 *How am I coming home?* Where am I in flow, allowing myself to be who I am—the full spectrum—without resistance yet with full participation in life? Where am I telling myself the truth and moving from that place of knowing?

Now that you have a sense of home base for yourself, and the unique way in which your own intuition moves in your life, let's bring it all together. How do we practically use our newfound connection to what is right in front of us, what we no longer miss, along with the power of our gut and heart's intuitional navigation system? The next practice can be applied to just about any life situation, in real time, using present-sight, and it makes use of all the key principles you have encountered in your travels through this book.

CULMINATION PRACTICE   Eight Steps for Opening to Your Blind Spots and Navigating from Your Intuition

To begin this exercise, as you're getting used to it, I suggest you select a particular issue you'd like greater insight on. Then work through the steps using that as the situation at hand. Soon enough, answering the questions related to these steps and taking the suggested stances will become second nature, and your inner knowing will assume an ever greater role in all of your choices.

1 *Listen to what's real, using mindful awareness— the tools of insight and practice.*
  What do you feel in your body as you consider a decision? Do you feel a strong "no" or "yes" that you

are ignoring? Chances are that's relevant information
· to listen to. If you can't tell whether what you're
experiencing is fear or not, take time and sit with
it. Notice the emotions, the thoughts, the feelings.
Your clarity will emerge as you give everything in your
experience the space to be here and to deliver its
messages to you.

2 *Tell yourself the truth as you listen—the tools of
honesty and vulnerability.*
As you acknowledge what you feel and all that is in
your experience, can you tell yourself any truth of the
moment? For example: *I feel hurt and angry. My sense is
that this marriage has reached a pivot point and we need
help trying to save it. I feel scared and I don't want to do
anything right now except hide.* The truth of the moment,
unveiled and unhidden from yourself, has the power to
work wonders. The naming of it will deeply relieve you
from the tension and struggle of holding it in.

3 *Act from your inner knowing as you tell yourself
the truth—the tools of discriminative wisdom and
empowered responsiveness.*
As you listen and tell yourself the truth, what do you
most know about this situation or about what you're
learning? What action is being called for in your life?
Acting from your inner knowing may mean taking no
action at all, but it's what you know to do, or not do.
It could mean having a conversation with someone, or
saying no where you're sure there is a "no." Remember
the idea that anything that isn't a 100 percent "yes" is
a "no." That can help clarify when you aren't listening
to your inner knowing. Acting comes from a place of
empowerment and strength but it also comes through
vulnerability. If it comes from fear, it may not reflect your
deepest knowing.

4 *Be comfortable with not needing a reason for your actions and decisions—the tool of surfing the unknown with self-confidence and trust.*

People will ask you to explain yourself. You can give them a reason if you want to, or you can give yourself permission to say, "I don't know. I have a sense that this is what I need to do." Watch for times when you know strongly and without a reason that you need to do something and then make up a reason for the choice so that you (or others) can feel comfortable with your decision. Let yourself *not* know why you do what you do. Of course, sometimes you'll be utterly clear about why you're making a given choice, but that won't happen all the time. Give yourself permission to not know, yet to still act. What a relief!

5 *Be comfortable with failure if your actions lead you astray—the tools of self-compassion and curiosity.*

Understand that part of the learning journey means you will fail, you will mess up, you will not say the right thing, and you will hurt others and yourself. When you understand that, you are far more willing to take responsibility for and learn from your actions than when you resist your mistakes. When you are in resistance, you will try to hide what you did wrong, try to push things through that don't need pushing anymore, and try to prove that you're right. Failure just means you are learning, and the more comfortable you are with the process, the better you will surf the waves.

6 *Let yourself off the hook from your "shoulds," your self-blame, the prison of your own mind—the tools of emotional intelligence and inquiry.*

Retire your loyal soldiers: your inner critic, the voice of "shoulds." Letting yourself off the hook from those harsh, judgmental voices allows you to let in where you betray yourself or another, or where you are blind and not listening. In not needing to be a certain way, you become who you are—a full-spectrum human being.

7 *Laugh at yourself and let go of taking yourself so seriously—the tools of awareness and humor.*
Place yourself in the context of history and think of all the love and war and birth and death that have come before you. See what a tiny point you are in the grand array of the world. Laugh at how you make such meaning of everything and feel that so much is at stake. Find the humor in the way you hold on, and in doing so, let go.

8 *Love what comes—the tools of compassion and welcoming.*
It's so easy to forget to love what comes. It's so easy to resist and refuse what life hands you. It's doing the simple thing of loving, with a welcoming presence, what arises in your life that changes everything. Love is the chief blind spot unlocker. It undoes our hatred, the way we blame and judge, and the way we don't listen well. Let love reside inside you and speak from your most profound depths. When we trust that we can take an aligned action in the world—any action that is spontaneous and relevant to the moment—it is easier to love because viewing through the lens of love doesn't threaten. We can love while we experience everything else under the sun. It seems to hold this whole thing together, doesn't it?

You have traveled far in your explorations of blind spots, how to uncover them, how to gain insights into them, and the myriad ways in which stepping from the shadows into the light can benefit your life and the lives of those around you. In the next chapter I offer a quick, concise guide to working with blind spots. Approach this guide with the mindful qualities of lightheartedness and curiosity, and you're likely to uncover your hidden gifts!

10

HAPPY TRAILS

A Concise Guide to Working
with Your Blind Spots

WITH YOUR JOURNEY through this book nearing its end, I trust that you have gained some insights into the unseen drives that motivate you to behave in ways that don't best serve your life. You may find yourself blinking *in* to your life, in a way that surprises you. Your blindness is receding and you've stopped missing what's right in front of you. Your blind spots may now be fully revealed, either through self-inquiry or the counsel of others. Or you are aware of a few elements you think *may* form part of a blind spot, but you can't see exactly what that hidden drive is. That's fine—you don't have to have it mapped out in a complete formulation; you can work with the glimmers of that shining gift and coax it further out of the dark.

Consider what we learned in chapter 1: that the visual blind spot in our eye keeps us from seeing that there is a small hole in our field of vision (we fill it in with corresponding detail). We have a blind spot but we can't see it; hence the name. It turns out that there's a simple exercise to help you physically see your own blind spot! Take a piece of paper and draw a small X on the right side, and 5 inches to the left, draw a dot the size of a penny (or do a Google search for "blind spot test" and you can do it on your computer). Hold the paper in front of you and close your right eye. Look at the X. Slowly move the paper toward your face and then away from it, and the dot will disappear at one particular point, and then reappear when you move the paper again. You can also flip it: place the cross on the left and the dot on the right, close your left eye, and stare at the cross with your right eye. When it disappears, that is where the place in your retina that doesn't have photoreceptor cells matches the dot on the paper. Voila, you've now "seen" your blind spot. Now you know, without a shadow of a doubt, that you do indeed have a blind spot.

However, just because you discovered it doesn't mean that you aren't at times smack dab in the middle of that blind spot without knowing it. Here is where our work comes in. We need help catching where and how our blind spots show up in our lives in order to stop missing what's been right in front of us all along and gain the gift of clear seeing. Knowing you have a blind spot is half the equation, and working to illuminate the various ways it shows up in your life is the other half—that is where you gain the gifts of empowerment, authenticity, and connection with your own wild aliveness. I will leave you with two effective ways to harvest the fruit of all your honest inquiry into the blind spots that hold you back.

PRACTICE Flip It for Good

I invite you to take some patterned behaviors and any attendant recycled emotions or core beliefs that you have recognized or that others have shared with you, and in a spirit of experimentation—and with as much lightness as you can muster—try working with them by walking through the following five steps. To help guide you through, let's take as an example this insight: "You try to find acceptance through proving your worth but you don't need to, and in fact it's annoying that you toot your own horn all the time."

> **1** *Flip it to find the gift:* Often we are seeking from others what we really need to give ourselves first. If you try to find acceptance from others, *flip it:* ask, "How am I not accepting *myself* as I am?" If you are trying to prove your worth to others, *flip it:* acknowledge your intrinsic worth *apart from what you do.* Can you see how this already starts bringing

forth the gifts hidden within the shadow? The gift is the power of your worth and your great capacity to meet and welcome yourself as you are. The inverse is often the key to unlocking a blind spot.

2 *Find where it's true:* Even if hearing a particular insight hurt, or it didn't resonate as a repeated blind spot in your life, look for places where sometimes, one part of you does that, thinks that, or feels that—like making sure your superiors at work hear about your accomplishments and congratulate you. When you can find a part of you that behaves and feels a certain way some of the time (even if rarely), you are getting close to the part of you that you may have disowned and that may be occupying prime blind-spot real estate. A blind spot does not have to be something you always do! This is key to remember.

And again, acknowledging that you sometimes operate from this drive doesn't need to define you. Maybe this comes out only at certain stressful times, like if you're worried you might lose your job. And if you were to see that this is the situation you happen to be in, you might not feel the need to try so hard to get others to see your worth.

3 *Look for connecting patterns:* What behavior, thought, or emotion has recurred that may be causing suffering in your life? Are there certain times when it happens, in certain instances and scenarios? Does it happen only with one gender, or with people who remind you of someone from your childhood? A tricky part here is that you're not trying to figure out a pattern analytically. Rather, you're looking for clues. Take a wide-lens view and see if you spot any patterns—and take your time. The power of beginning to notice and recognize these instances can be enough, and the resulting insights that spur your growth will come organically *as you live your life,* not necessarily through sitting down and "figuring it out" in your mind.

4 *Find your vulnerability:* When you illuminate what has been blind to you, how do you experience the vulnerability of being exposed? It may just be a feeling of tenderness or sadness in the body, or even one of openness. As children we were all so innocent in our desire for love and acceptance, and often that innocence felt stolen from us. It is in finding your vulnerability that you allow what is in the shadow to be present to you as it is: that powerful, primary portal to insight. In feeling your vulnerability, have kindness for yourself and perhaps say inwardly, *Bless my heart. When I couldn't stop talking about my accomplishments in that meeting, I was doing the best I knew how in that moment because I was blind to what was going on underneath.* Learn how it feels in your body to be both vulnerable and undefended and to listen for the gifts of being with what is, as it is.

5 *Illuminate the gift:* What forms of power, truth, aliveness, or authenticity are revealed when you pull back the curtain that's concealed your blind spot? To take the example of seeking outwardly for acceptance, perhaps you have denied your own irreplaceable and unique value in the world. When you acknowledge your intrinsic worth and let go of judging yourself so harshly, you may find yourself brimming with the authentic expression of truth, both inward and outward. If you have an underlying insecurity that causes you to blindly overmanage others or toot your own horn, what form of self-acceptance is being asked of you? Once you *give yourself* that acceptance, you may encounter a wild, alive essence in your way of navigating the world that, although unpredictable when compared to your patterns of blindness, is full of natural power and grace.

See to Know

Another way to inquire into your blind spots is to ask yourself the
following three questions and then explore the suggested solutions.

1 *What am I trading in?* Do I blame others in order to get
   acceptance? Hide my inner knowing to get connection?
   Withhold love to get love or avoid the truth to get safety?
   Solution: *Give yourself what you are trading in.*
   Take responsibility, acknowledge your inner knowing, give
   yourself love, tell yourself the truth. These will result in your
   getting what you want: accepting and relating to yourself,
   and feeling safe. Then you can truly receive those things
   from others.

2 *When I go blind, do I stop seeing myself, or do I stop
   seeing others?*
   Do I lose empathy and connection with others to be "right"
   or to defend an image of myself? Or do I lose empathy
   and connection with myself in order to please the other,
   out of fear that my voice won't be heard, or to stay safe?
   The foundation of this question is connection: Where do
   you shut down to protect yourself and go to sleep to your
   fully alive self? Where do you crowd the other out, or allow
   yourself to be crowded out?
   Solution: *Allow yourself to be seen. Allow the other
   to be seen.*
   Let go of the image you're defending. Be willing to
   have empathy for yourself or others.

3 Notice when you ask yourself things like *How could this
   happen? How could they do that? How could I have
   done that? How did I miss that?*
   These are all huge signs of a blind spot. You are likely
   not seeing something that has been right in front of you
   all along, out of a blind spot. This may protect you from
   having to deal with something you would prefer to avoid,

but in the long term it hurts you. Your work is to see what is there and admit what you know by drawing what you know into the light and taking responsibility for seeing.

Solution: Fill in these blanks: *This happened because _____. They did that because _____. I did that because _____. I missed that because _____.*

That way, you will let yourself know what you do know, even if it's hazy or unclear.

Illuminating blind spots is a journey into matters of the heart and our core beliefs and fundamental drivers. It's not about getting all the data right or getting a certain output after inputting all the variables correctly. In a sense, the output doesn't matter. What is hidden in the shadow is intelligent and it is on its own time frame—not ours—in emerging into the light. We are surfacing what hurts in us and what is stuck in us—*and what is most powerful in us*—and giving it some sunshine and presence. Happy trails to you, as you welcome yourself—shadow and all. In doing so, may you find yourself in flow, no longer missing what's right in front of you: your own unimaginably bright and free being.

AFTERWORD
The Biggest Blind Spot of All

> If the doors of perception were cleansed
> every thing would appear to man as it is, infinite.
> For man has closed himself up, till he sees all things
> thro' narrow chinks of his cavern.
>
> **WILLIAM BLAKE**[1]

WE ALL HAVE MOMENTS when the curtains part and we see no longer "through a glass darkly," but instead with utter clarity and conviction, something that is unmistakably true or real. It can happen when you're sweeping the kitchen floor, when you're thinking about what you will eat for dinner, or while you're wondering whether your niece is going to heal well from surgery. It can happen while you're sitting in silence in nature or on a retreat when your thoughts are still, or noisy. It can happen in the middle of a conversation, after you've finished a book, when you're gazing at your lover, or even in the middle of a fight. It can happen when a rock falls from your hand and hits the floor.

Moments of piercing insight occur in many different contexts and appear in many different forms. They may take the form of relative truths: *I need to marry this person* or *This job is over.* Or they could be more universal truths: *The Divine is inherently kind* or *I can let go now; I am held* or *I just discovered a new law about the universe!*

And then there are moments that bring a radical shift in perception, an essential awakening to who you are.

I had moved back home after several years outside the US, finishing college and living and working in Canada and Europe. I had just turned down acceptance to Hamburg University in Germany to get my master's in peace research and security studies. Here I was, living with my folks and trying to listen for the next direction in my life. Yes, I wanted to fix the world's problems, but it was dawning on me that I would have to focus on my own challenges first if I wanted to be of any real use. I had spent the day in the shade of a huge, tangled oak tree, working from my mom's back-porch home office. As dusk fell, I ran a bath and then soaked while finishing a book. I stepped out of the tub, wrapped myself in a towel, and lay down on my bed, staring at the wall. I am prone to staring at walls; to me they are like blank canvases that hold space for inner exploration, mind wandering, and resting without agenda.

I happened to be looking at a calendar on the wall, in an unfocused way. And then suddenly, out of nowhere, I recognized beyond any doubt that I *was* the calendar. There was no longer a "me" over here looking at the "calendar" on the wall.

I wouldn't have described it at the time in spiritual language that mystics have used throughout the centuries, such as: "Oh! Everything is one!" There was no verbal formulation at all, just pure recognition and pure seeing.

It was a radical shift in perception, appearing unbidden. And although paradigm-shifting, it was the most obvious and normal-feeling recognition in the entire world—I was not who I had always thought I was, and neither was the calendar, or anything else. It was unvarnished and beautiful in its revelation. This "truth" felt much closer, and simpler, and more amazing than anything I could have deliberately conjured up. It was clear as day. *Oh . . . of course! How have I not seen this before?* A blindfold had dropped from my eyes and I saw things just as they were, free of intervening narrative or perceptual clouds. Blake's doors of perception had opened and everything appeared as it was: infinite.

I got up and rushed to the bathroom mirror, without thought. Just to look. And the insight was confirmed. *Holy cow, I'm looking at myself from everywhere! I'm simultaneously me and everything, and as a result everything looks different and feels different and is different.* I could see everything.

While nothing had outwardly changed, borders and boundaries had dropped. I recognized that the body and mind that I took to be "me" and "mine" just was not what I had thought it was. I mean, I was *me*, but I *wasn't—my ideas weren't true.*

And in that moment of insight, the engine that generates all the beliefs that go along with "being someone" just stalled out. Kaput. My mind was quiet, amazed and in wonder and full of deep relaxation and equanimity. I was unable to believe a single thought because, although I could see the conventional truth in some of them, I saw through them immediately, and I was left with only an extraordinary silence, and with no capacity to believe a single thing that appeared. It felt like pure grace.

Many years later I found myself sitting in a red-cushioned booth at a Thai restaurant in San Rafael, California, across from John Prendergast, the mentor whom I mentioned earlier in the book. John and I had sat at this booth a lot over the years. I'd spent a decade integrating the fundamental shift in perception that had rocked my world back in my Ohio bedroom, and this time I was describing how, just days before while sweeping the floor, my sense of "self" completely fell away. It was a reprise on the same theme, yet it carried with it an unceremonious finality, like a ripened fruit falling to the ground, with no one around to notice. He gently listened, and then chuckled, his eyes misty and present. We sat together in a shared sense of presence as we spoke of the freedom that springs naturally from the heart when we finally let go in this way.

The familiar way I had been holding the world together, I told John, through the filter and organization my brain had so astutely created, had made another tectonic shift. What I was experiencing—in my own customized fashion, given my makeup and temperament—was seeing through the biggest blind spot of all: that we are separate from the world around us and that our ideas and stories are the truest things going. John, in his wisdom, quietly witnessed the moment together with me. After we shared a bit more together, he simply said, "Don't drive right away. Walk around the block a few times."

As I took his advice and ambled for a while, I felt like someone had blown up a balloon in my heart and all I could know was the beauty in the world. And at the same time, it was heartbreaking. I wish I had better words to describe it, but it's not an idea—to say anything at all about it is to make it something it's not. Experiences like these hack your biggest blind spot without trying, and without any mental framework. There's a reason all those Zen masters do crazy stuff like put a pair of shoes on their head and walk out the door when you ask them a question; they are demonstrating a fundamental insight into the nature of self (or no-self, depending how you look at it), and they have everything at their fingertips as props to help them make their point. It's like they've lost their sense of propriety and in so doing they are pointing out where you are still holding on to yours.

Those moments of awakening—while staring at the wall, sweeping the floor—helped me see what seemed *unequivocally* to have been right in front of me all along. But life's moments—99 percent of them—don't come as the poet David Whyte wrote in his poem "The Truelove," "so grandly, so Biblically." They come intimately, in a heartfelt conversation with a relative, at the turning of a door handle, at the glance of a child, at a moment at the hospital when you don't know which way it's going to go, walking up the same staircase for the thousandth time. They come when you're resting in your lover's arms and feeling how tenuous, beautiful, and fragile life is.

I had been completely blind to what was there all along. I kept seeing my thoughts, emotions, and what came and went in my visual and perceptive field as if they were the truest thing. In some way this was 100 percent accurate. But the blindness with which I was viewing them obscured a simpler form of seeing: that in no longer holding ourselves apart from the world, everything becomes simple, loving, with no inherent drama. And when we allow to drop away the armoring of the self that we take ourselves to be, we no longer need to navigate from an image, and life flows unhindered through us.

The implications of this for the global community are profound. When we are looking through these transformative doors of perception, it makes no sense to do war—because ultimately, there isn't anyone to go to war with: we are always meeting ourselves. As Thich Nhat Hanh has said many times, "Peace is every step." The more we wake up to this, individually and collectively—the more fully our biggest shared blind spot can be liberated from darkness and made evident in the bright light of day—the more precious each step becomes. We have no choice but to appreciate each moment and welcome whatever it contains. Irritation with a loved one, the evening light falling through the branches of the trees, the ordinariness, and the brilliance: the whole beautiful mess.

And just like this, we wake up together.

ACKNOWLEDGMENTS

I WROTE THIS BOOK in a vacuum, a bubble, and a cave, without much input other than from my editors and the Sounds True team, and a few baristas at my local café in Boulder, Colorado. That said, it's my mentors and friends who have shaped me and whose words are tucked neatly into so many of these pages. Thanks first to Jaime Schwalb, the associate publisher at Sounds True and someone I deeply admire, respect, and want to emulate: your wise, super smart, kind, insightful way of being is inspiring. Thanks for asking me, when I first met you over a sushi lunch, what kind of book I might write, were I to write one, and for supporting me from that day on in getting this project out to the world. Secondly, thank you to my first editor, Alice Peck, for telling me to keep writing, and reminding me of Anne Lamott's wise words about just getting the first shitty draft out and going from there. I love your quirky, brilliant, academic, caring, witty way. You shaped this book in the most respectful fashion. And thank you to my second editor, Sheridan McCarthy, who came along at the right time with the right frame of mind and heart to support the ideas in this book into their final form with grace and wisdom.

Thank you to my friends who believed in me. For my dearest friend, Anne Douglas, who helped me uncover the essence of this book on her sunny back deck in Banff, Canada, over a glass of wine. For Jeff Foster, for all your kindred spirit support; it's meant the world to me. For Michael Taft, because you seemed to mean it when you said you thought I could do this. I believed you. For my mentor and friend John Prendergast: thank you for all the years of sitting together and exploring the nature of things. Our friendship is a delight, and I appreciate you so much—the essence of this book has the fragrance of what we share together. For Richard Miller, whose words are embedded in these pages: I learned an incredible amount of what I know from you. Thank you for training me in meditation and helping me through what was the most difficult part of my journey. Without that, this book wouldn't be here. Thanks to Mario Galarreta, who asked me to go all the way with this book. To Fuyuko, James, Catherine, Loriel, Julia, Rich, Mark, Rick, Matt, Tamra, Kelly, Oli, Simon, Monique, and Tracey for your friendship and support. Thank you, Meng, for plucking me out of a crowd and introducing me to Google's world, and for being so curious all the time about everything. And Mirabai Bush, for showing me how to be a powerful woman in the coolest and most unassuming way.

To my family: Mom and Dad, thanks for being so simple, inside and out. For your humility and curiosity, and joy in seeing your kids flourish. For my siblings and their partners Brian, Sarah, Amy, Ben: thanks for pointing out my blind spots and for your support and love. And to everyone else who told me what I was missing that was right in front of me, whether they knew it or not. To my therapist, Paul: this book (and other good things in my life) certainly would not exist if it weren't for you and your insight.

Lastly, to everyone who reads this book: thank you! I sure hope it is of benefit.

NOTES

INTRODUCTION

1. Anne Lamott, "Cruise Ship," in *The Best Women's Travel Writing 2006: True Stories from Around the World*, ed. Lucy McCauley (Palo Alto, CA: Traveler's Tales, 2006), 34.

CHAPTER 1 ATTENTIONAL BLINK:
WHAT WE MISS AND HOW WE MISS IT

1. Charles Darwin, *The Expression of the Emotions in Man and Animals* (New York: D. Appleton & Company, 1872), chap. 12, https://brocku.ca/MeadProject/Darwin/Darwin_1872_12.html.
2. Anil Seth, "Your Brain Hallucinates Your Conscious Reality," TED Talk on YouTube, posted July 18, 2017, youtube.com/watch?v=lyu7v7nWzfo.
3. Wikipedia, S.V. "Blind spot," last modified September 28, 2017, en.wikipedia.org/wiki/Blind_spot. Also see Richard Gregory and Patrick Cavanagh, "The Blind Spot," Scholarpedia, August 1, 2011, scholarpedia.org/article/The_Blind_Spot.
4. Kimron L. Shapiro, Jane Raymond, and Karen Arnell, "Attentional blink," Scholarpedia, June 2, 2009, scholarpedia.org/article/Attentional_blink.
5. Jane E. Raymond, Kimron L. Shapiro, and Karen M. Arnell, "Temporary Suppression of Visual Processing in an RSVP Task: An Attentional Blink?," *Journal of Experimental Human Psychology: Human Perception and Performance*, 18, no. 3

(1992): 849–60, dc.uba.ar/materias/incc/2015/c2/practicas/
p1/raymond-1992.pdf.

6. Daniel Goleman, "How Self-Awareness Impacts Your Work," blog post, October 4, 2015, danielgoleman.info/ daniel-goleman-how-self-awareness-impacts-your-work.

7. Elissa Epel et al, "Can Meditation Slow Rate of Cellular Aging? Cognitive Stress, Mindfulness, and Telomeres," *Annals of the New York Academy of Sciences* 1172 (August 2009): 34–53, doi: 10.1111/j.1749–6632.2009.04414.x.

8. Heleen A. Slagter et al, "Mental Training Affects Distribution of Limited Brain Resources," *PLOS Biology Journal* 5, no. 6 (May 2007): e138, doi: 10.1371/journal.pbio.0050138.

9. Sara van Leeuwen, Notger Mueller, and Lucia Melloni, "Age effects on attentional blink performance in meditation," *Consciousness and Cognition* 18, no. 3 (September 2009): 593–99, doi: 10.1016/j.concog.2009.05.001.

10. Joshua D. Rooks et al, "'We Are Talking About Practice': the Influence of Mindfulness vs. Relaxation Training on Athletes' Attention and Well-Being over High-Demand Intervals," *Journal of Cognitive Enhancement* 1, no. 2 (June 2017): 141–53, doi: 10.1007/s41465-017-0016-5.

11. Daniel J. Simons and Christopher F. Chabris, "Gorillas in our midst: sustained inattentional blindness for dynamic events," *Perception* 28 (June 1999): 1059–74, chabris.com/ Simons1999.pdf.

CHAPTER 2 YOU SEE IT . . . BUT YOU DON'T SEE IT: DECODING THE STORIES IN OUR MINDS

1. Gelett Burgess, "The Purple Cow," in *Concise Oxford Dictionary of Quotations* (Oxford: Oxford University Press, 2011).

2. Daniel Kahneman, *Thinking, Fast and Slow* (New York: Farrar, Straus and Giroux, 2011), 43.

3. Matthew T. Gailliot and Roy F. Baumeister, "The Physiology of Willpower: Linking Blood Glucose to Self-Control," *Personality and Social Psychology Review* 11, no. 4 (November 2007): 303–27, doi: 10.1177/1088868307303030.

4. Kahneman, *Thinking, Fast and Slow*, 28.
5. Kahneman, *Thinking, Fast and Slow*, 31.
6. Daniel Kahneman, Jack L. Knetsch, and Richard H. Thaler, "Experimental Tests of the Endowment Effect and the Coase Theorem," *Journal of Political Economy* 98, no. 6 (December 1990): 1325–48, doi:10.1086/261737; and Kahneman, *Thinking, Fast and Slow*, 293.
7. S. A. Jackson, "Toward a Conceptual Understanding of the Flow Experience in Elite Athletes," *Research Quarterly for Exercise and Sport* 67, no. 1 (March 1996): 76–90, doi: 10.1080/02701367.1996.10608859.
8. Yi-Yuan Tang, Britta K. Hölzel, and Michael I. Posner, "The neuroscience of mindfulness meditation," *Nature Reviews Neuroscience* 16, no. 4 (April 2015): 213–25, doi: 10.1038/nrn3916.
9. Kahneman, *Thinking, Fast and Slow*, 42.
10. Kahneman, *Thinking, Fast and Slow*, 43; and Gailliot and Baumeister, "The Physiology of Willpower."
11. Rainer Maria Rilke, *Rilke's Book of Hours: Love Poems to God*, trans. Anita Barrows and Joanna Macy (New York: Riverhead Books, 1996), 58.

CHAPTER 3 SHORTCUT TO FLOW STATE: HACKING FAULTY INTUITIONS

1. Mihaly Csikszentmihalyi, *Finding Flow: The Psychology of Engagement with Everyday Life* (New York: Basic Books, 1998), 13.
2. Attributed to Confucius by Henry David Thoreau, *Walden* (1854), Amazon Classics edition (Seattle: Amazon Publishing, 2017), 8.
3. Kahneman, *Thinking, Fast and Slow*, 81, 129, 199–203.
4. Kahneman, *Thinking, Fast and Slow*, 25; and Michael Lewis, *The Undoing Project: A Friendship that Changed Our Minds* (New York: Norton, 2016), 184.
5. Kahneman, *Thinking, Fast and Slow*, 75.
6. Kahneman, *Thinking, Fast and Slow*, 138, 142.

7. Gerd Gigerenzer, "Dread risk, September 11, and Fatal Traffic Accidents," *Psychological Science* 15, no. 4 (April 2004): 286–87, doi: 10.1111/j.0956-7976.2004.00668.x.

8. Kahneman, *Thinking, Fast and Slow*, 133.

9. Kahneman, *Thinking, Fast and Slow*, 346.

10. Kahneman, *Thinking, Fast and Slow*, 201.

11. Gerd Gigerenzer, *Gut Feelings: The Intelligence of the Unconscious* (New York: Penguin Books, 2007), 33; and S. L. Beilock and T. H. Carr, "On the fragility of skilled performance: what governs choking under pressure?," *Journal of Experimental Psychology: General* 130, no. 4 (December 2001): 701–25, doi: 10.10.1037//0096-3445.130.4.70 1 1.

CHAPTER 4   CHOOSE YOUR OWN ADVENTURE: DISCOVERING PERSONALIZED CORE BELIEFS

1. David Whyte, *When the Heart Breaks: A Journey Through Requited and Unrequited Love,* audiobook (Boulder, CO: Sounds True, 2013).

CHAPTER 5   THE FULL SPECTRUM: WELCOMING EMOTIONAL BLIND SPOTS

1. Carl G. Jung, *C. G. Jung Speaking: Interviews and Encounters,* ed. William McGuire and R. F. C. Hull (Princeton, NJ: Princeton University Press, 1977), 452, archive.org/stream/ MemoriesDreamsReflectionsCarlJung/carlgustavjung-interviewsandencounters-110821120821-phpapp02#page/ n237/mode/2up.

2. Mary Oliver, "The Summer Day," *New and Selected Poems,* vol. 1 (Boston: Beacon Press, 1992), 94.

CHAPTER 6   LOVE IS BLIND: FIRST IMPRESSIONS AND FALLING IN LOVE

1. K. Daniel O'Leary et al, "Is Long-Term Love More Than a Rare Phenomenon? If So, What Are Its Correlates?," *Social Psychological and Personality Science* 3, vol. 2 (August 5, 2011): 241–49, doi: 10.1177/1948550611417015.

2. Helen Fisher, "The Drive for Love: The Neural Mechanism for Mate Selection," in Robert Sternberg and Karin Weis, eds., *The New Psychology of Love* (New Haven: Yale University Press, 2006), 87–107, fusiondotnet.files.wordpress.com/2015/02/15npolve.pdf.

3. Fisher, "The Drive for Love," in Sternberg and Weis, eds., *The New Psychology of Love*, 91.

4. Fisher, "The Drive for Love," in Sternberg and Weis, eds., *The New Psychology of Love*, 99.

5. Michael Winnick, "Putting a Finger on Our Phone Obsession," dscout.com, June 16, 2016, blog.dscout.com/mobile-touches.

6. Kahneman, *Thinking, Fast and Slow*, 292–93.

7. Fisher, "The Drive for Love" in Sternberg and Weis, eds., *The New Psychology of Love*, 102.

8. Kahneman, *Thinking, Fast and Slow*, 210–11, 219.

9. Kahneman, *Thinking, Fast and Slow*, 82.

10. Kahneman, *Thinking, Fast and Slow*, 211.

11. Kahneman, *Thinking, Fast and Slow*, 201.

12. Kahneman, *Thinking, Fast and Slow*, 82, 85.

13. Matteo Forgiarini, Marcello Gallucci, and Angelo Maravita, "Racism and the Empathy for Pain on Our Skin," *Frontiers in Psychology* 2 (May 23, 2008):108, doi: 10.3389/fpsyg.2011.00108.

CHAPTER 7   SELF-COMPASSION . . . AND THE BIG REVEAL

1. Haruki Murakami, *Norwegian Wood*, trans. Jay Rubin (New York: Vintage, 2000), 100.

CHAPTER 8   F*CK FEEDBACK: ILLUMINATING HOW OTHERS SEE US

1. Emily Dickinson, letter to Thomas Wentworth Higginson received April 26, 1862, in *The Life and Letters of Emily Dickinson* (New York: Biblo-Tannen Publishers, 1971), 239.

CHAPTER 9 TRUST YOUR GUT: UNCOVERING YOUR INTUITIONAL NAVIGATION SYSTEM

1. Gigerenzer, *Gut Feelings*, 103.
2. Gigerenzer, *Gut Feelings*, 94, 98, 103.
3. Gigerenzer, *Gut Feelings*, 6.
4. Gerd Gigerenzer, interviewed by Justin Fox, "Instinct Can Beat Analytical Thinking," *Harvard Business Review* (June 20, 2014), hbr.org/2014/06/instinct-can-beat-analytical-thinking.
5. Gigerenzer, *Gut Feelings*, 80.
6. Gigerenzer, *Gut Feelings*, 16.
7. Gigerenzer, *Gut Feelings*, 7–8, 28–29.
8. Gigerenzer, *Gut Feelings*, 33, 55, 135.
9. Leslie Valiant, *Probably Approximately Correct: Nature's Algorithms for Learning and Prospering in a Complex World* (New York: Basic Books, 2013), 14.

AFTERWORD

1. William Blake, *The Marriage of Heaven and Hell* (1794; Mineola, NY: Dover, 1994), 36.

ABOUT THE AUTHOR

KELLY BOYS is the host of *Mindfulness Monthly*, an online training and practice community dedicated to exploring mindfulness in daily life. Kelly graduated from university in British Columbia, Canada, with a degree in intercultural religious studies and is a mindfulness trainer and consultant. She has worked at Google, in prisons and veterans' centers, and with United Nations humanitarian workers in the Middle East delivering mindfulness programs. She teaches retreats at spots like the Esalen Institute. Kelly lives in Marin County, California.

ABOUT SOUNDS TRUE

SOUNDS TRUE is a multimedia publisher whose mission is to inspire and support personal transformation and spiritual awakening. Founded in 1985 and located in Boulder, Colorado, we work with many of the leading spiritual teachers, thinkers, healers, and visionary artists of our time. We strive with every title to preserve the essential "living wisdom" of the author or artist. It is our goal to create products that not only provide information to a reader or listener, but that also embody the quality of a wisdom transmission.

For those seeking genuine transformation, Sounds True is your trusted partner. At SoundsTrue.com you will find a wealth of free resources to support your journey, including exclusive weekly audio interviews, free downloads, interactive learning tools, and other special savings on all our titles.

To learn more, please visit SoundsTrue.com/freegifts or call us toll-free at 800.333.9185.

SOUNDS TRUE
many voices, one journey